COME
TO THE
COW
PENS!

COME TO THE COW PENS!

THE STORY OF THE BATTLE OF COWPENS
JANUARY 17, 1781

PROSE AND POETRY BY
CHRISTINE R. SWAGER

ILLUSTRATIONS BY
JOHN ROBERTSON

2002

Second printing, January 2004

Book & cover design–Mark Olencki
Front cover & title page image—Battle of Cowpens by Charles McBarron,
     Courtesy of Cowpens NB
Printed by McNaughton & Gunn, Inc., Michigan

Library of Congress Cataloging-in-Publication Data

Swager, Christine R., 1930-
 Come to the cow pens! : the story of the Battle of Cowpens, January
17, 1781 / by Christine R. Swager ; illustrations by John Robertson.
      p. cm.
Summary: Follows the course of an important Revolutionary War battle and
profiles Brigadier General Daniel Morgan and other figures using both
prose and verse.
Includes bibliographical references,
 ISBN 1-891885-31-6 (alk. paper)
 1. Cowpens, Battle of, Cowpens, S.C., 1781–Juvenile literature.
[1. Cowpens, Battle of, Cowpens, S.C., 1781. 2. United
States–History–Revolution, 1775-1783–Campaigns.] I. Robertson, John,
ill. II. Title.
 E241.C9 S93 2002
 973.3'37–dc21
                              2002015221

Hub City Writers Project
Post Office Box 8421
Spartanburg, South Carolina 29305
(864) 577-9349 · fax (864) 577-0188 · www.hubcity.org

Publication of *Come to the Cow Pens!*
is made possible through the generous
contributions of the following:

Anonymous

Battle of Cowpens Chapter, Daughters
of the American Revolution

Kate Barry Chapter, Daughters
of the American Revolution

Wilhelmina Dearybury

Georgia Society, Sons of the American Revolution

Daniel Morgan Chapter,
Sons of the American Revolution

Town & Country Garden Club of Cowpens

Introduction

Come to the Cow Pens! is a thrilling story of the American Revolution in South Carolina. Mixing poetry with prose, Dr. Christine Swager has written yet another delightful book for young adults.

Beginning with the settlement of the backcountry by thousands of Scots-Irish immigrants and continuing through the horrors of the brutal war in the Carolina backcountry, Dr. Swager's book fairly crackles with action. Why men chose to fight for America and against their king has been the subject of literally hundreds of historical works. In *Come to the Cow Pens!* the poetic voice of a backcountry settler explains the reason quite simply in the first chapter: "This land belongs to me."

The American Revolution in South Carolina was a nasty, bloody struggle between Patriots (or Partisans, who fought for America's independence) and Tories (or Loyalists, who fought for the King). It was a war of neighbor against neighbor; of brother against brother; and father against son. It was sometimes said that the only thing a man could trust was his rifle—any other weapon or any person might betray him.

After the fall of Charleston in May 1780, the British assumed that they had successfully reconquered South Carolina. Within less than two months they discovered otherwise at the Battle of Williamson's Plantation (or Huck's Defeat) on 12 July. From that day onward, the partisans of South Carolina mounted a relentless and ferocious campaign against the British army of occupation and their Tory allies.

Some historians tend to denigrate and underestimate the role of the Partisans (such as Francis Marion, Thomas Sumter, William Hill, William Bratton, and Andrew Pickens) and say that it was the Continental Army that won the Revolution in South Carolina. That simply is not true. Without the whipping that the Partisans put on Lord Cornwallis' army in the six weeks after Huck's defeat, there would have been no crucial Battle at King's Mountain. And, after King's Mountain, the Partisans continued to harass and defeat the army of occupation at every turn. Then came the Battle of Cowpens. The battle was fought by Continental troops and Partisan bands. In the battle plan, which Daniel Morgan developed, the Partisans played a critical role. The result was a tremendous victory for the American cause. After Cowpens, the British Army straggled out of South Carolina into North Carolina and to defeat at Yorktown.

The nature of the warfare was such that men came and went. Few were in their partisan bands all the time. The Partisans were true citizen-soldiers who responded to their country's need when there was an enemy threat. When there was none, they returned home to their families and their fields.

In *Come to the Cow Pens!* Dr. Swager presents to the reader a stirring account of these citizen-soldiers and gives them the credit they are due for helping our nation win its independence.

Walter Edgar
George Washington Professor of History
University of South Carolina

1

SCOTS-IRISH SETTLEMENT

Until the early 1700s Native Americans, primarily the Cherokees, inhabited the backcountry of the Carolinas. Most white settlers to these new colonies had populated the area close to the coast from what is now Maine to Georgia. There were some exceptions. A few intrepid explorers and fur traders had intruded into the Indian country, and there was some friction between them and the Indians.

In the early 1700s the situation changed. Germans, who had suffered religious persecution in their homeland, were encouraged to come to this new country and many did. South Carolina became home to many who settled in the area between the Saluda and Broad Rivers, in Saxe Gotha. But it was the immigrants from Ireland who would make the greatest impact on the backcountry of the Carolinas.

Between 1700 and the time of the Revolutionary War, a quarter of a million (250,000) people sailed from Ulster in Ireland to the new colonies. We refer to them as Scots-Irish, and many people today in the Carolinas trace their ancestry to these settlers.

Before 1700 England had encouraged large numbers of Scots to emigrate to Ireland to establish linen and woolen industries. The industrious Scots had been so successful that their linen and wool competed with the English merchants. Alarmed, these English merchants pressured the British Parliament to levy taxes and import restrictions on the goods from Ireland. At the same time, Irish landlords greatly increased the rents the Scots had to pay for their homes and property. These conditions imposed great hardships on the Scots.

However, the event that impelled thousands to leave Ireland was related to their religious freedom. Scots Presbyterians had never been assimilated into the Irish Roman Catholic society. They remained very much apart from the Irish. The Scots Presbyterian Church and its clergy were central to their lives. When England enacted laws that required all officers in the Army, all officers of the court, and all who officiated at legal functions be members of the established Church of England, this infuriated members of other religious groups. The law would, in effect, make marriages and baptisms performed by Presbyterian clergy null and void. The Scots living in Ireland could no longer tolerate this affront to their religion, and they left in great numbers. In some cases whole congregations with their clergy left Ireland and came to America seeking religious freedom where they could practice their faith.

Since many—about 100,000—did not have the money to pay for their ship passage, they made arrangements to come as indentured servants. Their passage would be paid, and they would work off the debt with a specified number of years' service. Then they would be free of the debt and ready to establish themselves in this new country.

Most of the immigrants arrived at the New England ports and found that the land nearby was settled or too expensive. They moved to the south along the Great Wagon Road, which stretched from Philadelphia to Savannah, Georgia. The road went from Philadelphia down the Shenandoah Valley of Virginia, south to western North Carolina, then into South Carolina. At the Waxhaws, an area near the North Carolina border, the road branched, with one fork going south through Camden, and the other, west to the foothills and Augusta. At first the trail was merely a path for walkers and their oxen or horses. With time and many travelers, the trail became broader and could accommodate carts and wagons.

The Scots-Irish moved down the Great Wagon Road to the south because land was plentiful and cheap. The area was uncrowded, and they looked for places to establish homes and families. Some travelers moved with relatives and friends. Occasionally, entire congregations of Presbyterians moved south together.

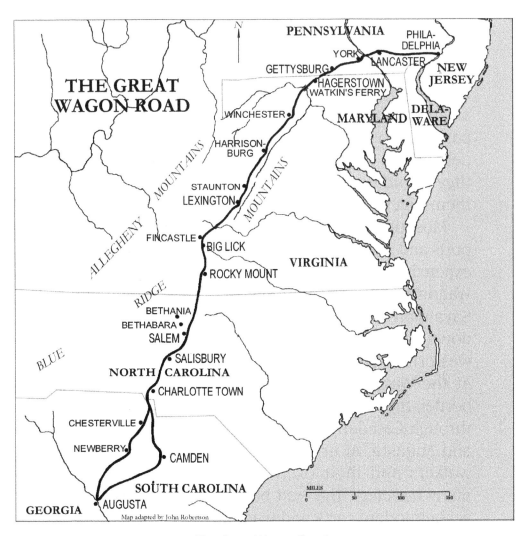

The Great Wagon Road
(After Rouse, 1995)

Some stopped in Virginia and established families. Their sons and daughters would later move south. Many moved directly to the Waxhaws and established a Presbyterian Church there. Then some of those moved farther west. As areas were settled, the Scots-

Irish moved to western Carolina and, when Georgia became part of the colonies in 1752, they moved into north Georgia. Some were adventurers, but all wanted homes. They had come from a background where ownership of property was unlikely and they had been at the mercy of the landholders.

They had left an area of religious persecution and looked for a place where they could worship as they chose. In the Carolinas the lands beyond the fall of the rivers, the foothills and upcountry, were available to Protestants of any persuasion. Here they could practice their beliefs without interference.

In the old country they had seen their profitable linen and woolen production ruined by government intervention. In the upcountry of the Carolinas they were beyond the reach of the coastal plantation owners and their political interference.

In the lands they had left behind, Scotland and then Ireland, these settlers had never owned the land. They were at the mercy of the landed gentry from whom they rented their homes. Here, in this new country, they would own their homes. This sense of ownership was possibly the most compelling reason they chose to face the hardships of a pioneer life. It may have been a primitive home, but it was theirs.

See the hills there in the distance
Far as the eye can see.
This is Carolina country
And this belongs to me.

From the crowded ports of Ulster
In a stinking ship at sea
I have traveled ever westward
And this land belongs to me.
Down the Wagon Road I struggled
Through the German pastures green,
On the bottom land of rivers
Sure, the richest land I've seen.
But in western Carolina
Rivers rush and wild game roam
Trees reach forever skyward
It is here I'll build my home.
Here my cabin will be safe
For my wife, my babes and me,
Here I'll die and I'll be buried
For this land belongs to me.

The first sites occupied were those that could provide water for the household and cattle, a rushing stream capable of powering a gristmill, and trees for lumber. Until a shelter was built, the settlers were at the mercy of the elements.

Since the settlers traveled in groups of family, friends, or church congregations, there were a few neighbors to help erect shelters. Logs were cut and notched, and neighbors assembled for a "log rolling" as they lifted the logs for the walls into place. The settlers had brought with them only some essentials: a rifle, an axe, an iron cooking pot. They had what they or their horse, mule, or oxen could carry. All else had to be fashioned from what was available in the wilderness. Beds, tables, and chairs were built from saplings, and spoons, scoops, dippers, and bowls were carved from the abundant wood. Sometimes a stone fireplace would be built, and flooring laid over the dirt.

In warm weather foods were prepared over an open fire outside. Game was plentiful, and the settler could provide meat for his family if he was a good shot. Since the rifle had to be reloaded after every shot, hunters became expert shots, or their family went hungry for meat.

The native peoples who had roamed this land for centuries were not pleased with these new settlers. White trappers and hunters who had roamed the Indian territory had been temporary—these new settlers were building cabins, and they intended to stay. This alarmed the Cherokee and led to some attacks on the settlers living on the frontier.

To protect themselves against Indian attacks the settlers erected "forts," which were really stockades around some cabins that were conveniently located. Here families gathered when danger threatened. However, not all settlers escaped the wrath of the Indians, and the attacks led to many casualties. Tragically, the settlers were determined to stay. Whatever the hardships, whatever the costs, they were not to be displaced again. This was home.

I've cleared the land for planting,
Built a cabin strong of pine.
Although the heart is heavy
With the loss of kin of mine.
I'll build the cabin stronger
To protect family and me
Here I'll die and here be buried.
This land belongs to me.

2

DANGER IN THE BACKCOUNTRY

Life for the settlers in the backcountry of the Carolinas was dangerous in the early days of colonization. First, there had been the threat of Indian attacks and the terrible consequences. Then, with the advent of the Revolutionary War, different dangers emerged.

The Revolutionary War began in 1775 when settlers in America rebelled against England because they were being taxed by the British Parliament in which they had no representatives. The cry was, "No taxation without representation," but that fell on deaf ears in London. King George III was determined to put down what he saw as a threat to his authority. The war in America initially was fought mostly in northern provinces and along the border with Canada, another British colony.

On 28 June 1776 the British attempted an invasion of South Carolina. The British Navy shelled Sullivan's

Island near Charleston. The palmetto logs of the fort (now called Fort Moultrie) resisted the shells, and the British, unable to take the fort, withdrew. They lost interest in the south and concentrated their efforts in the northern colonies.

By the late 1770s the war had come to a stalemate. The British attempts to confront George Washington's Continental Army and defeat it had failed. In London frustration grew over the long war, which had cost dearly in terms of money and casualties. The British Parliament devised a plan to move British troops from the northern colonies to the southern colonies. They believed that it would be an easy task to conquer Georgia and the Carolinas because there were many British supporters in the south. Then, they would move into Virginia and force the Americans to cease their resistance. This new plan was called the Southern Campaign and, at first, it was very successful.

The British Navy landed soldiers on the coast of Georgia. Savannah fell to the British on 29 December 1778. With Georgia occupied, the British troops moved on to South Carolina and laid siege to Charleston. On 12 May 1780 Major General Benjamin Lincoln, commander of the Continental Army at Charleston, surrendered the city and an American force of 5,500 to the British. This would be the largest surrender of troops of the United States until World War II.

British troops then moved into the interior of South Carolina to Camden and occupied that town. On 16 August 1780 British forces under the command of Lord

Cornwallis defeated another American army under the command of Major General Horatio Gates at the Battle of Camden. Now, British troops occupied the entire state and established British outposts to control the territory.

There were many settlers who wished to remain with England and were loyal to King George. They were known as Loyalists, Tories, or King's men. These Tories were organized into militia units and authorized by the British to "keep the King's peace."

Other colonists were eager for the colonies to be free of England and to establish a new country. These were known as Whigs, Partisans, or Patriots. Of course, the English considered them rebels. In the upcountry the people were divided in their loyalty, and all felt very strongly about their allegiance. Neighbors, who were once united against the Indians, now became bitter enemies and fought each other.

By 1780 the settlers were still living in log cabins and were growing crops for their survival. The rich pasture lands provided forage for cattle, and large numbers of cows roamed the area. Occasionally, drovers would herd the cattle and drive them to markets in Charleston, Camden, or farther north to Philadelphia. The cow pens at the intersection of the Green River Road and the Island Ford Road in the South Carolina backcountry were well known. That was a location where cattle were grazed and gathered for the drive to markets.

Yet the families were not safe, especially in the

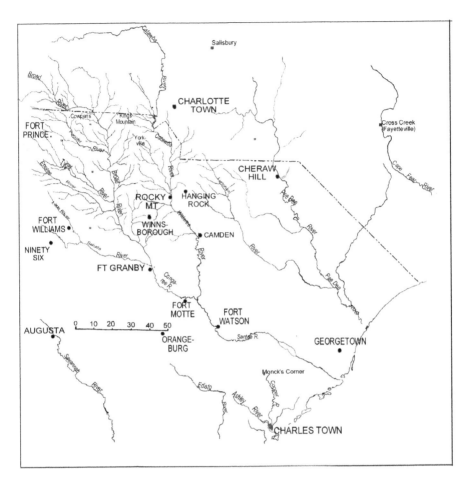

British outposts in South Carolina

backcountry of the Carolinas. The Indians had been allies of England and were still conspiring with the British to attack and subdue the Patriots. Wolves roamed the area, so the settlers and their cattle were often threatened. Only their vigilance kept them from being prey to marauding Indians, wild animals, and the neighboring Tories. This was the life of the settler in the backcountry of the Carolinas just before the Battle of Cowpens, the most significant battle in England's Southern Campaign of the Revolutionary War.

January 1781 was a bitterly cold month. The winter rains had soaked the earth, and every river, branch, and creek flooded over the banks, making travel difficult. In those days, ferries over some of the larger rivers made the expanse passable but, on the smaller branches and creeks, travelers had to ford, or wade, the icy waters.

> Through the uplands, down the hollows
> Do you hear the wind a-howlin'?
> Deer are fleeing to the deep woods
> For tonight the wolves are prowlin'.
>
> Cold is seeping through the log chinks,
> Through the windows, 'round the door,
> And the bitter chill is rising
> From the cabin's earthen floor.
>
> Come and hunker by the fire,
> Catch the warmth as best you can.
> We'll share our perlow in the pot,
> And the cornbread in the pan.
>
> Danger threatens in the uplands—
> Not the Indians as before,
> Now it's Tories who would kill us
> In this bloody, brutal war.

Yes, there's danger in the mountains.
Evil lurks and foes are near.
Eat a bit and rest, my friend,
For tonight, there's safety here.

The British victory at Camden in August had given the local Tories great encouragement. Emboldened by the British success and support, they retaliated for past mistreatment by the Whigs. There had been great dissension in the upcountry, and now the level of violence escalated. Bloodshed and brutality increased. Settlers were no longer safe in their own homes as enemies roamed the area, punishing all who opposed them. It was a bitter civil war with neighbor killing neighbor. Nowhere in the country was it more bitter

A militiaman responds to a call to arms.

Robert Scruggs' log cabin
(Courtesy, Cowpens National Battlefield)

than in the upcountry of South Carolina.

Lord Cornwallis, the commander of the British troops in the Southern provinces, had established his headquarters in Camden. As he surveyed the line of British outposts across the state and his supply lines from Charleston to those outposts, he was confident that the campaign was successful. Thinking that the British control was complete in South Carolina, Lord Cornwallis decided that it was time to implement the next phase of the campaign, a thrust through North Carolina to Virginia. He gave the Camden area command to Lord Rawdon and with 2,200 soldiers headed north.

In spite of Lord Cornwallis' confidence that all was under British control, there was opposition to the British occupation. Though the defeat of the American troops at Camden had disheartened some Patriots, Francis Marion (known as "the Swamp Fox") and Thomas Sumter had taken to the field and rallied Patriot forces to oppose the enemy. Several encounters had inflicted serious damage on the British troops and on Tory militia. As the British moved inland, their lengthening supply lines were vulnerable to attack. Francis Marion, operating along the supply line from Charleston to Camden that followed the Santee River, had disrupted the British supplies to the interior.

Lord Cornwallis seemed confident that Lord Rawdon could defend the British positions in the Camden district and moved north to the Charlotte, North Carolina, area where he established his headquarters. Wanting to capitalize on the enthusiastic support of

Chicken Perlow *(upcountry)*
Chicken Prileau *(lowcountry)*

Fill iron pot half full of water and hang pot over a brisk fire. When the water boils, add a chicken (or fowl) and cook until flesh is tender. Remove chicken and remove flesh from bones when cool enough to handle. In boiling water add onions, garlic and seasonings as available. Stir in about two pounds of rice and cook over fire, stirring when necessary to prevent burning or sticking. Return chicken to the pot. Cook till liquid is absorbed.

~Annie Puckett, 2nd. South Carolina, cook

Lord Charles Cornwallis as he would have appeared during the Southern Campaign of the American Revolution *(Pencil drawing by John Robertson Jr. from Gainesborough portrait)*

Tories that had followed his great victory at Camden, Lord Cornwallis directed a young Scots officer, Major Patrick Ferguson, to move out along the western border between North and South Carolina and recruit Tories into the British Army. Hundreds of Tories living in the upcountry joined him and were trained as British soldiers. However, Ferguson wanted even more recruits, and he sent word to the men in the mountains. He demanded that they come and join him or he would cross the mountains, hang them, and burn their homes.

The mountain men were used to hardship. Their numbers had been increased by refugees from the western Carolinas and northern Georgia. Many of the refugees had fought against Tories and British and had fled their homes to escape reprisals. They had long fought Indians to protect their homes and families and did not intend to give in to Ferguson's threats. These men, often called "overmountain men," were determined to stop Ferguson before he could move into their territory. They rode across the mountains in the bitter cold of late fall and gathered at the cow pens in the upcountry of South Carolina. The cow pens area was a landmark known by all who traveled in the upcountry.

The mountain men camped at the cow pens on the Green River Road on the night of 6 October 1780. These men were not soldiers but settlers. However, they were not inexperienced in combat. They had fought Indians for years and were dressed for frontier fighting. They wore leggings, moccasins, hunting shirts, and were armed with long rifles, tomahawks, and scalping knives. Although a loosely organized force, there were men among them who had commanded militia units and were highly respected by these men who had assembled to eliminate the threat to their families. The men were organized in groups and commanders were selected.

On the morning of 7 October 1780 the men broke camp and rode to King's Mountain where Ferguson was encamped. The mountain men surrounded the mountain and, carrying shot in their mouths to assuage thirst and to be better able to reload their rifles rapidly, they started up the mountain. Ferguson commanded his troops in the manner of eighteenth-century fighting: The men fired their muskets on command and then, with bayonets fixed, charged their enemy. The mountain men did not stand firm to take the charge. They moved up and down the mountain firing from the cover of trees and rocks. Surrounded, the British had to move to counter the

Battle of King's Mountain, 7 October 1780
(1859 engraving from Alonzo Chappel painting. Courtesy, South Caroliniana Library)

threat as group after group of Patriots moved further up the mountain. Finally, Ferguson was killed, and his remaining troops surrendered. The mountain men had dealt the British a terrible blow. Including killed, wounded, and prisoners, the British had lost 1,000 men. This was hailed as great news to the citizens of occupied Carolina.

Were you there at King's Mountain
Where our riflemen so skilled
Taught the foe a bitter lesson?

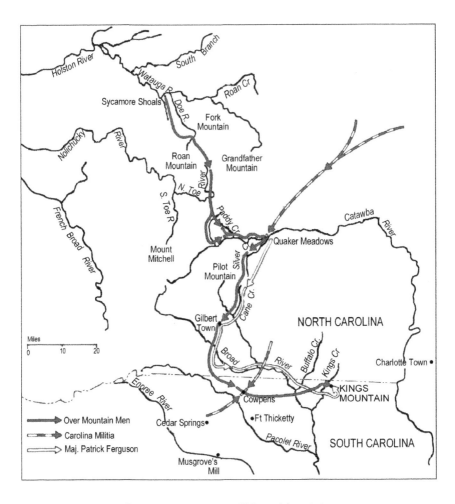

Route to the Battle of Kings Mountain
(After National Park Service)

Where Ferguson was killed?
They thought our men were cowards,
That they wouldn't fight, but run
In the face of British muskets
And the bayonet on the gun.
But the yelling boys kept moving
Up the slopes toward the fray,
And they didn't stop their shootin'
Till they had won the day.

At the time of the American victory at King's Mountain, Lord Cornwallis was still in his headquarters in Charlotte. After the death of Ferguson and the disastrous loss of 1,000 men at King's Mountain, the British commander realized that his western flank was exposed. Although most of the men he lost at King's Mountain were local Tories and a few were regular troops from the British outpost at Ninety-Six, that loss presented a problem. The Tories were local Carolinians, and their defeat was a bitter blow to British support. Tories, who had been encouraged at the British success at Camden, now realized that the British protection was powerless against the determined Whigs.

Perhaps now Cornwallis realized the extent of the opposition to British occupation. He certainly knew he had, to his west, in the upcountry of the Carolinas, mountain men who could fight and would fight. King's Mountain had proved that.

Lord Cornwallis moved his headquarters back

to Winnsboro, South Carolina, closer to British strongholds in Camden and Ninety-Six. As he retreated to Winnsboro, the winter rains had made the roads almost impassable. The British lost much equipment to the weather and many men to disease. Cornwallis himself was so ill he had to be transported in a wagon. It was a very rough ride.

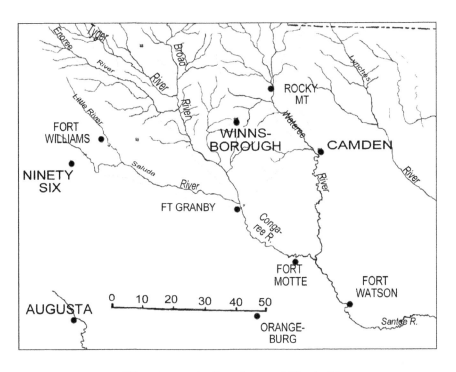

Winnsborough, Camden, and Ninety Six

3

MAJOR GENERAL NATHANAEL GREENE

While Lord Cornwallis was moving back to Winnsboro to strengthen his position, decisions were made in Congress that would impact the activity and safety of the settlers in the Carolinas. After the defeat of Major General Horatio Gates at the Battle of Camden, it was apparent that the Southern Army needed a new commander. The appointments Congress previously made had not been successful. The first commander had lost Savannah and Georgia. The second commander had lost his army to the British at Charleston, and the third commander had lost a costly battle at Camden.

Perhaps Congress was now wise enough to realize its errors, or perhaps its members just did not want to take the blame for another poor choice of a commander. In any case, they now did what they probably should have done in the beginning. They gave General George

Washington, Commander of the Continental Army, the authority to appoint a commander of the Southern Army. Washington appointed a man in whom he had great confidence, Major General Nathanael Greene.

Nathanael Greene was born in Rhode Island in the summer of 1742 into a Quaker family. His father owned a farm and iron works. The elder Greene not only espoused the Quaker philosophy of non-violence, he also thought hard work was more honorable than higher education, so Nathanael's formal education was minimal. Nat Greene worked on the farm and at the iron works, but he read voraciously. A young man of amazing intellect, he read on a wide range of subjects, but his great interest was history, especially military history. An early biographer writes of a "superior mind" and "Herculean memory."

After his father's death, Nathanael drifted away from strict obedience to the religion of his family and was removed from the Meeting of the Society of Friends (Quakers). He opposed the Quakers'

Nathanael Greene, 1742-1786
(Painted by Charles Wilson Peale, from life, 1783. Courtesy, Independence NHP)

disinterest in higher education as well as the pacifism.

In 1774 Greene married and the same year helped organize the Rhode Island militia. He was not selected as an officer possibly because he was handicapped by a stiff knee. Nathanael limped noticeably. Despite that, he was diligent in his military duties.

After the Battle at Lexington in 1775, the Rhode Island militia was assigned to Boston, and Greene was appointed by his state as commander and commissioned as a brigadier general. It was near Boston at this time that he met General George Washington. Greene had no battle experience, but Washington was impressed at the intellect of this new officer. Mrs. Washington and Mrs. Greene became friends, and the two families socialized when the ladies were in camp. General Greene attended Washington's councils of war and came to distrust the decisions of such councils. It would appear that he had a broad vision of strategy, but he needed experience.

Although George Washington and several of his officers had served in the British Army in protecting the American colonies in the French and Indian War, Greene was not one of the participants. Therefore, at the time of the American Revolution, he had no military experience. In spite of this, he accompanied Washington in this latest campaign and learned rapidly from his successes and failures. Washington came to value his keen intellect and extensive knowledge, and Greene saw more and more action as the war escalated. He saw action against the Hessians, German mercenaries who fought for the British, at Trenton and experienced the bitter cold of the winter camps.

In the winter of 1777-1778, Washington's winter camp was at Valley Forge. The situation was desperate as men suffered from cold and lack of clothing and food. Medical supplies were needed as the army was on the verge of annihilation from disease and starvation. Washington charged Greene with the task of providing supplies. This required stern measures, but Greene was equal to the task and provided the camp with some relief. Congress realized that a competent quartermaster general was needed, and Greene was nominated for the post.

Greene's ambition was to distinguish himself as a field officer, a fighting man. This new responsibility would remove him from the line, and he felt he would never make his mark in history as a quartermaster general. However, he realized that the intense suffering of the men at Valley Forge had been due to lack of proper supplies and he reluctantly took the appointment.

The job of the quartermaster was to acquire supplies of food for the army, forage for horses, uniforms, ammunition, arms, and all the accouterments of war and, having acquired them, transport them to where they were needed. It may have been a thankless job, but here Greene's vast knowledge of geography and his relentless attention to detail would enable him to excel.

Although now an administrative officer, Greene still hankered for action, and General Washington twice called him back for field duty. At Monmouth Court House on 28 June 1778, Greene had a field command. The British commander was Lord Cornwallis. The British attacked and met unexpected resistance from Greene's men who manned the guns and fired in volleys. Lord Cornwallis was repulsed and, no doubt, surprised by this professional encounter. Lord Cornwallis and General Greene would meet again, far from Monmouth Court House, in the interior of the Carolinas.

When Washington finally was authorized to appoint a new commander for the Southern Army, he appointed Major General Nathanael Greene on 14 October 1780. Greene was ordered to move to General Gates' headquarters as quickly as possible.

Greene had never been in the south, but it is a certainty that he had gathered all the information about the area and the events that had occurred there. Before he even arrived in Charlotte to take command, he had started reconnaissance of the area south of the Dan River on the North Carolina-Virginia border with special interest in the road and river systems. He needed an intimate knowledge of the terrain and the possibilities for moving supplies.

As dismal as the situation had been in the south, there was some good news. As Greene traveled south from Philadelphia, he learned of the victory at King's Mountain. Word of Greene's coming soon spread among the war-weary inhabitants of the Carolinas.

We have a new commander
Major General Nathanael Greene.
He's new to the Carolinas
But successful he has been
As the quartermaster general
He kept Continentals armed and fed,
And he's been in every battle
That George Washington ever led.
Finally, Congress has listened
To what Washington has to say.
And those politicians decided
To let George have his way.
He picked this former Quaker
(Greene forsook their peaceful laws)
And he's coming south to help us
Win our Patriot cause.
They say he's not the sort to run,
He's in the south to stay.
We'll outsmart Lord Cornwallis
And win, if Greene has his way.
So listen for your country's call
Keep handy powder, shot and gun
We'll help Greene do to Cornwallis
What we did to Ferguson.

General Greene's first concern was the condition of the army. It was poorly clothed, miserably fed, and inadequately armed. The American position was dismal, but Greene had already devised a strategy. He had not only acquired information about the terrain in which he would operate, but had gathered considerable intelligence about the conditions in the south and the position of Lord Cornwallis.

General Greene was well acquainted with the partisan activity in the Carolinas. He now wanted to coordinate the activities of the leaders who had kept the opposition alive. He sent Lt. Col. Henry Lee (Light Horse Harry) and his Lee's Legion to the swamps of the Santee to take the field with Francis Marion. Greene's intent was to increase the pressure on Lord Cornwallis by attacking the British outposts with such regularity that British troops could not be transferred from one point of conflict to another. With Marion attacking in the Pee Dee and Santee River areas and Sumter's men moving in the piedmont, the British outposts would be cut off.

Greene understood the necessity of maintaining supply lines, and he contemplated Lord Cornwallis's position. Francis Marion had already made the supply route from Charleston to Camden along the Santee River too dangerous for the British. The route now was from Charleston to Orangeburg, then to Friday's Ferry on the Congaree. Although this allowed supplies to move to Winnsboro, it put the columns on the wrong side of the Wateree River so that supplies would have to be ferried across the Wateree to Camden.

If the British used the river systems to transport supplies, they had to contend with great swampy areas

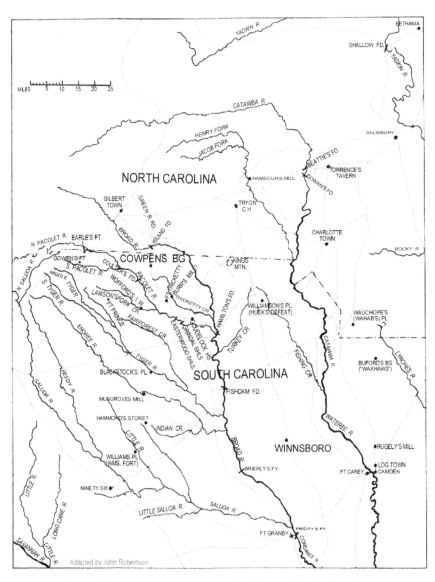

South Carolina backcountry and adjacent North Carolina
(After Babits, 1993. Courtesy, Dr. Bobby Gilmer Moss from his annotated Journal of Capt. Alexander Chesney)

that allowed mounted Patriots to attack and disrupt. Also the movement of supplies from Charleston to the interior required the British to move supplies upstream, against the currents. Greene's supplies would be coming downstream with the current. That did not escape Greene's notice.

General Greene was aware of Lord Cornwallis' supply difficulties, and he intended to increase the pressure. As the British moved farther from their resupply base at Charleston, the problems would increase. Greene intended that Francis Marion and Lt. Col. Lee would see to that.

Greene had information that targeted another serious weakness of the British. Although Lord Cornwallis had won battles, he had difficulties that Greene saw as potentially fatal. The climate in the Carolinas had not been kind to the British troops. Many of the units were provincials, troops recruited in the northern provinces—Americans who were regular British forces. Those men, along with the few British who had come from Europe, were unaccustomed to the rigors of life in the Carolina summers. By late August 1780, there were 800 soldiers in the hospital in Camden too ill for duty. Another outpost, at Cheraw, was incapacitated by illness.

Further, at the Battle of Camden, the Patriots initially inflicted serious casualties on the British forces, despite being eventually routed. Lord Cornwallis had lost twenty percent, or one in five, of his men on the field. Those soldiers would be impossible to replace.

Every dead British soldier diminished the threat, and every wounded or sick British soldier put a drain on the medical, food, and military supplies. Greene determined to inflict as many casualties on the British as possible while building his own army to fighting strength.

To implement his plans he needed a field commander who could and would press the enemy hard. He needed a commander who knew no fear and could inspire troops to fight. He needed a commander who understood his strategy and had the tactical abilities to implement it. He had that commander in Brigadier General Daniel Morgan.

When Greene replaced Major General Gates, Brigadier General Daniel Morgan was part of that command and was operating in western Carolina. Greene certainly knew the experience and capabilities of this colorful officer and wanted Morgan to figure prominently in his plans. When, in early December, Morgan reported to his new commander, Major General Nathanael Greene, a union was forged that dramatically impacted the upcountry of the Carolinas.

It was an unlikely pairing: Greene, the cerebral, and Morgan, the cantankerous; Greene, the student of war, and Morgan, the practitioner of war.

General Greene needed time to rebuild the Southern Army while keeping a threatening posture toward the British. To do this, Greene split his forces into two commands. Part of the army he kept himself

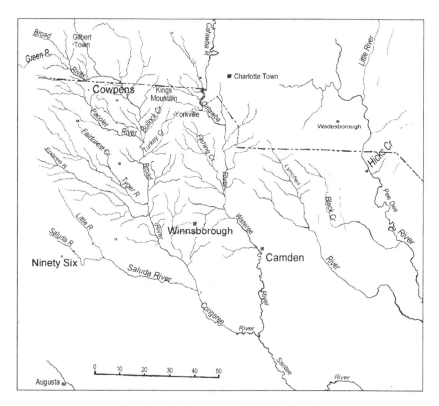

Carolina backcountry to Hicks Creek

and moved toward the Cheraws, where he could be more easily re-supplied from Hillsboro. He established his camp by Hicks Creek on the Great Pee Dee River across the river from the present town of Cheraw.

The rest, under the command of Brigadier General Daniel Morgan, he sent into western Carolina. Here it would be easier to feed the troops and to provide forage for the horses than in the Charlotte area, which had been picked clean. It also threatened Cornwallis' position at Winnsboro and kept the British from moving north again.

Lord Cornwallis saw the danger. If he tried to move north toward Virginia he would leave two factions of the Continental Army behind him. If he moved against Greene, Morgan would be at his back, and if he moved toward Morgan, Greene would not only be behind him but in a position to move on Charleston. For a time, Lord Cornwallis gathered intelligence on the movements of the enemy and prepared to respond to the danger.

For intelligence, Lord Cornwallis depended on fast-moving mounted troops, the dragoons, or light infantry commanded by Lt. Col. Banastre Tarleton, an infamous commander and a great favorite of Cornwallis. It would be this officer who would have to check Morgan's advance when the time came. It was not long in coming. The cast of characters that would lead to the battle at the cow pens was in place.

4

BRIGADIER GENERAL
DANIEL MORGAN

Brigadier General Daniel Morgan was a colorful character. Little is known of his early life or of his family. He was probably born 1735 or 1736 in New Jersey of Welsh immigrants. The circumstances and size of his family are unknown. That he had little education was evident. He could read and write but, in his youth, was often described as semi-literate. Certainly he did not acquire the polish expected of gentlemen of that era until later in his life.

Morgan appeared in Pennsylvania in the winter of 1752 and joined a group of travelers moving south on the Great Wagon Road. Morgan, however, only traveled as far as the Winchester area of western Virginia and stopped to work. Still only in his teens, and without family, he had to make his own way. After working at other jobs, he finally was offered a job as a wagoner. Since all the supplies had to cross the Blue Ridge

Mountains by wagon, it was a profitable business. Morgan determined to own his business, and within two years he had saved enough to buy a wagon and team. Now, at twenty, Daniel Morgan traveled the wilderness roads and became familiar with an ever-widening area.

Morgan was a man of importance. He was widely known as one having a quick wit and good humor to his friends, but a fierce fighter to his enemies. He was tall and through his hard work had developed great muscular arms and shoulders. He lived a rough life among rough settlers and was a hard drinker, a gambler, a carouser, and a brawler. At barely twenty he was an independent wagoner, and it was a life he enjoyed. That independence soon was interrupted when, in 1754, the French moved down from Canada to threaten British sovereignty. The French defeated a Virginia militia unit commanded by George Washington who had tried to drive them back. The British commander, Major General Braddock, arrived in western Virginia and needed wagons to transport his supplies. Morgan first transported supplies back and forth over the primitive roads, but then was impressed or drafted to accompany the army.

British officers had little respect for the independent colonists, and Daniel Morgan had no respect for authority. He once took offense to a British officer's behavior and hit him, knocking him unconscious. He was sentenced to a whipping of 400 lashes on the bare back with a cat o' nine tails. It was brutal punishment, and when the whipping was over, his flesh hung in shreds, and his boots were full of blood. Such a beating would have killed many men, but Morgan survived. He always maintained that he had remained conscious throughout the ordeal and had counted the blows. He insisted that his tormentor had miscounted and he only suffered 399 lashes. He often joked that "old King George" owed him one more strike.

The Braddock Campaign ended in disaster as the column was ambushed by a French and Indian force. The European style of fighting was no match for the brutality of the frontier, and the British suffered tremendous casualties, including Braddock himself. Morgan emptied his wagon of supplies and destroyed them to carry wounded men to safety. Braddock died on the retreat and was buried in the wagon trail so his body would not be found and mutilated by the enemy. It is said that Morgan's wagon was one of the convoy that was driven over the grave to obscure it.

Weeks later Morgan joined a ranger company to protect the frontier. In April 1756 Morgan and another ranger were ambushed by Indians. His companion was scalped and Morgan seriously wounded by a bullet through his neck and cheek, knocking out several teeth. When most of the Indians stopped to scalp his companion, Morgan wheeled his horse and headed back to safety, sixteen miles away. An Indian followed, expecting the seriously wounded Morgan to fall from his horse, but Morgan retained his seat in the saddle and escaped. Although he recovered from that wound, his face was seriously scarred.

When George Washington disbanded the rangers in October 1756, Daniel Morgan returned to civilian life, his back and face scarred for life. He was barely twenty-one years old.

Daniel appeared to resume his old lifestyle. He was known as the best horseman, the fastest runner, the fiercest fighter, and strongest wrestler. He enjoyed the boisterous life around Battletown in western Virginia as he resumed wagoneering. He was said to have had knowledge of the road systems surpassed by no other.

Romance entered his life in 1761 when he met and courted young Abigail Curry, who was then in her late teens. When the two settled down to family life, Abigail exposed her new husband to education and religion. She is credited with Morgan's increased level of literacy in his later years and his conversion to the Presbyterian faith. Two daughters were born in the 1760s, and Morgan's life became centered in his farm. His traveling became more limited. As the farm grew, Morgan needed more help, and by 1774 he had acquired ten slaves.

Many Virginians had pushed into the Ohio Valley in violation of the treaty that England had forged with the Indians. When the Indians began to retaliate, Morgan became involved with the militia in Virginia as they built stockades to protect the settlements and to patrol the area. When the governor of Virginia wanted volunteers to enter the Ohio territory to fight Indians and destroy their villages, Morgan joined the small group. Morgan was so successful in his encounters that he gained a reputation as an Indian fighter, a superb rifleman, and a forceful leader.

When the revolution against England became a reality and Congress asked Virginia to provide a company of expert riflemen from the western counties, Daniel Morgan was elected captain. The unit would join the Continental Army in Boston. The riflemen were dressed in hunting shirts, leggings, and moccasins. They carried tomahawks and scalping knives along with their long rifles. They immediately were assigned duty against the British at Boston Neck, and the Virginians made the trip from western Virginia to Boston in twenty-three days. These men were unlike any the Bostonians had ever seen, but it did not take the British long to learn about the prowess of these Virginians and their rifles.

Camp life was not palatable to the Virginians. They demonstrated their marksmanship to the other soldiers with target practice, but they dismayed commanders by brawling. When Washington planned an assault on Canada and included rifle companies, Morgan volunteered his men, and they were selected. The expedition commander was Colonel Benedict Arnold, and the route initially took them up the Kennebec River in Maine. They had to portage, or carry, the boats and supplies around rapids and across the high interior as they made their way to the St. Lawrence River. Morgan led the way, clearing trails, guiding bateaux (boats) through icy waters, and portaging the rough terrain. It was a bitterly cold trip, but the march was successful. The attack on Quebec, however, was not, and Morgan was taken prisoner. He was returned to America in August 1776 in a prisoner exchange; later he returned to Virginia and was reunited with his wife and daughters.

However, the war was not over for Daniel Morgan. With a commission as colonel, Morgan was on the road again in western Virginia, recruiting men for the 11th Virginia Regiment. It would be an elite unit, and Morgan wanted only expert shots. To this group were eventually added 500 picked Continentals who wore hunting shirts and carried long rifles. Morgan now had an independent command. Although this unit saw action in the northern provinces, it would be at Saratoga where Morgan made his greatest contribution yet.

In 1777 British General John Burgoyne marched an army from Canada towards Albany, New York, in hopes of winning the war. Colonel Daniel Morgan accompanied the American Army to help stop Burgoyne's advance. Again he served with Benedict Arnold. The general officer with the responsibility of stopping Burgoyne was Major General Horatio Gates.

General Burgoyne had disdain for the American Army and contempt for the militia, citizen soldiers. He certainly underestimated his adversaries. After a disastrous encounter with militia at Bennington,

Burgoyne met the American Army at Freeman's Farm, the first battle of Saratoga. As the British marched into the open field, sharpshooters fired from trees and treetops. In the long battle that ensued, the call of the wild turkey was heard again and again as Morgan signaled his riflemen. They shot British gunners as they tried to load and fire the artillery and targeted British officers who were attempting to command the infantry operation. In addition to the riflemen there were American Continentals with musket and bayonet, and they fought bravely. When darkness fell, the British were still on the field, but they had 700 men dead or wounded, many of them officers.

The British held on for a few more days and tried to advance but were stopped again. Burgoyne surrendered his force of 4,000 regulars on 17 October 1777. General Burgoyne had altered his opinion of the American soldier's ability to fight, and he complimented Colonel Daniel Morgan on the finest ranger regiment in the world.

The Battle of Saratoga was the turning point of the war in the northern colonies, but it would not be the only pivotal battle for Daniel Morgan. General Washington recalled Morgan to command rangers in the mid-Atlantic states. Morgan's men harassed the British columns under General Clinton's command.

After the Battle of Monmouth Courthouse, with the war at a stalemate, Daniel Morgan tendered his resignation to Congress and headed home to Winchester and his family. Although Burgoyne knew the value of

Daniel Morgan, the American Congress did not and had not promoted him to the rank of brigadier general, which he richly deserved. Embittered by the lack of promotion and plagued with the pain of sciatica and rheumatism from the punishment his body had taken through the years, Morgan left the service.

Morgan's recuperation was never complete but, in spite of his painful disabilities, he rejoined the Army after the disastrous Battle of Camden and moved south with a commission, finally, as brigadier general to join his old commander from Saratoga, Major General Horatio Gates.

Soon after Morgan joined his old friend, Congress removed Gates from the command of the Southern Army and replaced him with Major General Nathanael Greene. Now Morgan would serve under this new commander. In Morgan, Greene had a proven leader in combat, a man he could trust to carry the war to the enemy, a man who would not back away from danger.

When Greene divided his army and sent Daniel Morgan off to the west, he had complete trust in the experience and capabilities of his   famous rifleman. Although there was an attempt to keep in contact, the greater the distance the armies moved apart, the greater the problems of communication. Greene, who tended to oversee every detail, was giving command authority to Morgan.

The army that Morgan now commanded was referred to, by Greene, as the Flying Army. It was a hit and run operation, and no one knew that tactic better than Daniel Morgan.

Daniel Morgan, much as he must have appeared at Cowpens (Trumbull's portrait, engraved by J. F. E. Prud'homme)

We hear Dan'l Morgan's moving
To take Ninety-Six, they say.
The hero of Saratoga, comin' here—
I hope he'll stay.
We need him in Carolina
Before the Tories kill us all.
When Morgan's riflemen fire
British officers will fall.
Yes, we need Dan'l Morgan,
Lest we perish in this fray.
We need the "Old Wagoner."
Pray God he comes this way!

The units that accompanied Daniel Morgan as he moved to western Carolina were well chosen for the task assigned them. These were neither inexperienced nor poorly trained troops. They had faced the enemy and knew the smell of gun-

William Augustine
Washington,
1752-1810
*(Painted by Charles
Wilson Peale, from life,
in early 1780s. Courtesy,
Independence NHP)*

powder, the stench of death, and the exaltation of their own survival on the battlefield.

Perhaps the most illustrious group was the Continental Dragoons commanded by Lt. Col. William Washington, a relative of General George Washington. William was a colorful figure, described as tall, strong, and courageous. He had twice before fought Tarleton, and both times had been humiliated. He had twice been wounded in battle and would be again before the war was over. He was a warrior, and he was ready to fight again. However, his unit, numbering about eighty, was seriously undermanned.

Lt. Col. John Eager Howard, who commanded the Continental Infantry, had earned the reputation of a capable and courageous officer. The infantry included men from Maryland, Delaware, Virginia, and North Carolina who were enlisted for three years' duty. In addition, there was a company

John Eager Howard, 1752-1827
(Painted by Charles Wilson Peale, from life, in early 1780s. Courtesy, Independence NHP)

of Virginia State troops who served longer than militia and were considered to be better trained. There were about 300 men under Howard's command. Many were survivors of the disastrous affair at Camden, and some Virginians had survived Buford's Massacre in the Waxhaws.

Perhaps some of the men had fought with Morgan before with the Virginia sharpshooters at Boston Neck, or pushed their way up through Maine on that disastrous trip to Quebec. Some may have been with the Virginia rangers who shot down Burgoyne's British army at Freeman's Field at Saratoga. Whether they had fought with him before or not, they knew the mettle of Daniel Morgan. With so few Patriot victories in this lengthy war, the hero of Saratoga was widely known, and his exploits were legendary. Morgan was big and strong, quick to anger, and disinclined to back down from any threat. He was a soldier's soldier, and he wore leggings and a long, fringed rifle shirt, the garb of the backcountry rifleman. He was one of them.

The Flying Army with about 500 men moved west from the Charlotte area, and the chase began. Morgan's task was to discourage the Tories from overt support of the British and to "spirit up" the Patriots in the upcountry. Morgan was not a man on the defensive. He was ready to take the war to the Tories and to the British if they opposed him.

Morgan's force was small compared to British forces available to march against him. He would need more men, and he called for the militia to join him.

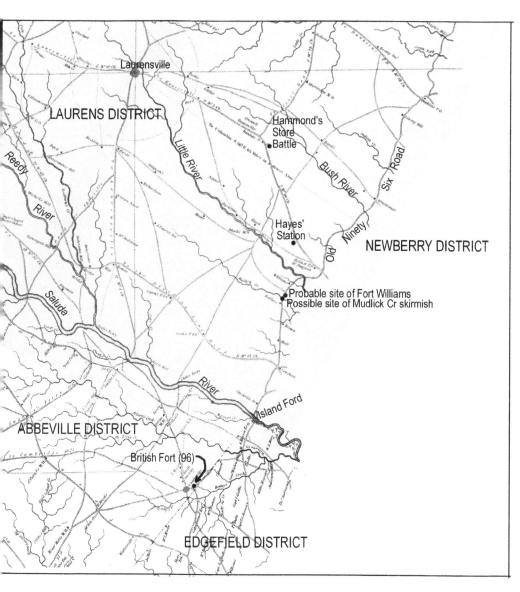

Proximity of Ninety Six, Hammond's Store, Fort Williams, Hayes' Station, and Mudlick Creek. Fort Williams was 15 miles from Ninety Six. *(Composite map made from three Mills Atlas maps, around 1820)*

While Morgan made his headquarters at Grindal Shoals on the Pacolet River, he ordered William Washington's cavalry to attack toward Ninety-Six. Washington's cavalry of about seventy-five was joined by 200 local mounted militia. At Hammond's Store they located a force of about 200 Georgia Tories who were marching to join the British at Ninety-Six. In a surprise attack, Washington inflicted over 150 casualties on the Loyalists and took forty prisoners. The Patriots suffered few casualties. Morgan's mission to "spirit up" the Patriots and intimidate the Tories had begun in earnest.

The Flying Army could move about the upcountry and raid successfully as Washington had done, but Morgan knew that his presence would not go unchallenged. He was right.

5

Adversaries

As Lord Cornwallis gathered intelligence at his headquarters in Winnsboro, he became more and more alarmed at Morgan's travels in the western Carolinas. It appeared that Morgan was threatening Ninety-Six, a very important British post in the upcountry. The British supporters, the Tories, were vulnerable, as Washington's attack on Hammond's Store proved. Morgan would have to be stopped.

Morgan had a very small force compared to the British army at Winnsboro. However, Lord Cornwallis dared not move the entire force toward Morgan, leaving Major General Greene and that part of the Continental Army at his back. He would have to divide his army, sending part of his force against Morgan. To command that force he selected Lt. Col. Banastre Tarleton, the commander of the British Legion. Cornwallis believed Tarleton to be the finest cavalry officer in the British Army.

Banastre Tarleton was the son of a British merchant. He was accustomed to wealth. He attended university at Oxford, where he was a lackluster student, and then decided to study law. He is reputed to have spent more time gambling in the gaming houses in London than in serious study. His inheritance was dissipated, and his mother bought him a commission in a British cavalry unit. This was usual in that time. One bought a commission, and the price was not cheap. This system meant that the officers in command in the British Army were of wealthy families, the ruling class. It also meant that, in case of a class struggle, the Army would support the King and the nobility. The more senior the commission, the more expensive, so the senior officers were, for the most part, either extremely wealthy or had patrons who were.

In 1776 Tarleton left his original unit and sailed to America with Lord Cornwallis. He was involved in South Carolina in the British attempt on Sullivan's Island. Returning to New York, Tarleton volunteered for duty with dragoons and quickly made a name for himself as fearless and aggressive. Promotions followed, and he was given command of the British Legion, a unit of mounted and infantry. The British Legion was a provincial unit; that is, the unit was recruited from among the supporters of the British in the New York area. Tarleton was one of the few Englishman in the unit, but he was the commander.

The Legion soon got a reputation for plunder and brutality that was excessive even in those bloody times. Tarleton had no inclination to prevent his men from committing such atrocities. After all, he was an Englishman of the upper class, and he held the American colonists as beneath contempt. In Tarleton's view, the Americans were resisting the authority of the King, and no punishment was too harsh for such rebels.

Tarleton saw much action in the northern colonies, and his reputation for daring and brutality grew. When the British Southern Campaign was implemented, Tarleton and his troops boarded ship and sailed to the south. In South Carolina Tarleton's Legion was especially effective in actions around Charleston, but it was after the Battle of Charleston that Tarleton was tagged with a name that followed him throughout the rest of the war.

In May 1780, a group of Virginia cavalry under the command of Colonel Buford was attempting to return north after hearing of the fall of Charleston. Tarleton and his troops caught the Virginians at the Waxhaws. Although details are sparse, it appears that Buford, knowing he was beaten, surrendered his troops. Tarleton's troops sabered to death 113 Virginians and badly wounded 150 after they had laid down their arms.

Buford's men had called for "quarter," a term signifying the accepted treatment of prisoners of war. When Tarleton's men slaughtered prisoners, Tarleton became known as "Bloody Tarleton," or "Bloody Ban," and the cry of "Tarleton's quarter," became

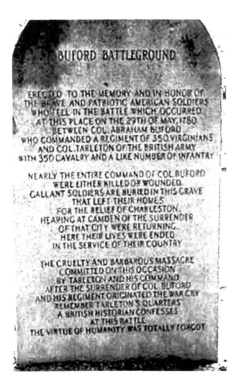

BUFORD BATTLEGROUND

ERECTED TO THE MEMORY AND IN HONOR OF
THE BRAVE AND PATRIOTIC AMERICAN SOLDIERS
WHO FELL IN THE BATTLE WHICH OCCURRED
AT THIS PLACE ON THE 29TH OF MAY, 1780
BETWEEN COL. ABRAHAM BUFORD
WHO COMMANDED A REGIMENT OF 350 VIRGINIANS
AND COL. TARLETON OF THE BRITISH ARMY
WITH 350 CAVALRY AND A LIKE NUMBER OF INFANTRY

NEARLY THE ENTIRE COMMAND OF COL. BUFORD
WERE EITHER KILLED OR WOUNDED.
GALLANT SOLDIERS ARE BURIED IN THIS GRAVE
THAT LEFT THEIR HOMES
FOR THE RELIEF OF CHARLESTON.
HEARING AT CAMDEN OF THE SURRENDER
OF THAT CITY WERE RETURNING.
HERE THEIR LIVES WERE ENDED
IN THE SERVICE OF THEIR COUNTRY

THE CRUELTY AND BARBAROUS MASSACRE
COMMITTED ON THIS OCCASION
BY TARLETON AND HIS COMMAND
AFTER THE SURRENDER OF COL. BUFORD
AND HIS REGIMENT ORIGINATED THE WAR CRY
"REMEMBER TARLETON'S QUARTERS"
A BRITISH HISTORIAN CONFESSES
AT THIS BATTLE
THE VIRTUE OF HUMANITY WAS TOTALLY FORGOT

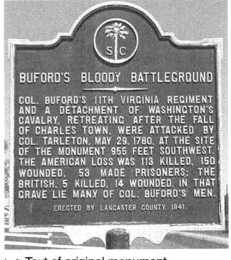

BUFORD'S BLOODY BATTLEGROUND

COL. BUFORD'S 11TH VIRGINIA REGIMENT
AND A DETACHMENT OF WASHINGTON'S
CAVALRY, RETREATING AFTER THE FALL
OF CHARLES TOWN, WERE ATTACKED BY
COL. TARLETON, MAY 29, 1780, AT THE SITE
OF THE MONUMENT 955 FEET SOUTHWEST.
THE AMERICAN LOSS WAS 113 KILLED, 150
WOUNDED, 53 MADE PRISONERS; THE
BRITISH, 5 KILLED, 14 WOUNDED. IN THAT
GRAVE LIE MANY OF COL. BUFORD'S MEN.

ERECTED BY LANCASTER COUNTY. 1841.

Left: Text of original monument.
(Relative strength of forces is in error.)

Above: SC historical marker at site

Below: Mass grave believed to contain
85 bodies. Another is believed to be
nearby containing 25 additional bodies.

a rallying cry for the Patriots. "Tarleton's quarter" meant no mercy, and the cry had been heard on King's Mountain as the mountaineers gained the summit. Violence breeds violence, and the brutality in the south escalated.

Now Tarleton had orders to hunt down and destroy Morgan, and the units under his command were seasoned soldiers. Tarleton's force would include his own British Legion Dragoons and the British Legion Infantry. These units were raised in Pennsylvania and New York of American citizens who supported the King. In addition, there were former Continental soldiers who had been captured at Charleston or Camden and who chose to enlist with the British rather than spend the rest of the war in prison ships. There were about 250 men in each unit, a total of roughly 500 men, who had accompanied Banastre Tarleton on his campaigns. They were provincial troops, but they were experienced and had the reputation for viciousness.

In addition to the British Legion Dragoons, there were about fifty mounted soldiers of the 17th Light Dragoons. This unit had served in America since they landed at Boston in 1775 and were now attached to the British Legion. These, too, were men of experience in warfare.

The 7th Regiment of Foot, or the Royal Fusiliers, was another unit of regulars. They had been in America since 1775 and had seen much action in the northern provinces before coming south. There were about 175 infantry in this unit, but many were recent replacements and were the least experienced of the troops.

The 71st Regiment of Foot, Highland Scots, or Fraser's Highlanders, had been recruited in Scotland for service in America. That unit had arrived in America in 1776 and had seen service in the north before coming south. They had fought at Savannah, Charleston, and Camden and deserved their designation as an elite force. There were about 260 infantrymen in this unit.

In addition, Tarleton had two small artillery pieces, 3-pounders, so called because they fired a three-pound projectile. They were also called "grasshoppers" because they recoiled after firing. There were about thirty artillerymen who accompanied Tarleton to service those guns.

Tarleton's total force numbered about 1,050 soldiers, aided by perhaps fifty Tory scouts. The leader of

Banastre Tarleton, 1754-1833
(Engraving from a portrait by Reynolds.
Courtesy, SC State Museum)

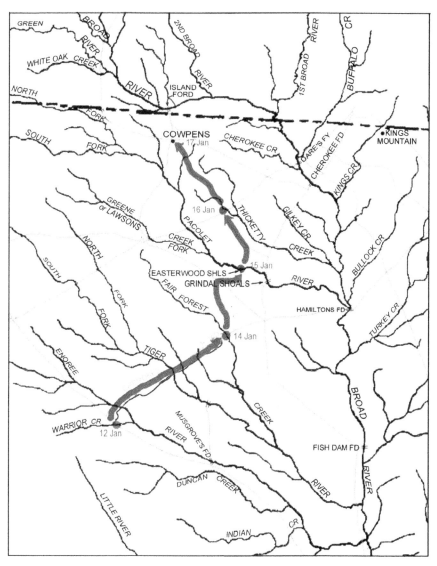

Tarleton's route to Cowpens
(After Army War College, 1928, and Moncure, 1996)

the scouts, Alexander Chesney, was a local Tory and knew the area well.

Although Tarleton's force was experienced, there was dissension. Many of the officers had been in military service since before Tarleton was born and resented the favoritism Lord Cornwallis had shown for the twenty-six-year-old cavalry officer. The more experienced officers resented Tarleton's rapid promotion through the ranks, and most of them in this command detested him. They not only deplored his brutality and his lack of control over his plundering troops but also doubted his ability for such a command. It was felt that his rashness would overcome sound judgment. The events would prove that their concerns were well founded.

To move toward Morgan would not be an easy task. The upcountry was rugged and unforgiving. The river systems were extensive, and few crossings were available. The winter rains had drenched the upcountry, and all the creeks and rivers were running high. Many rivers would have to be forded, and the men would have to wade through icy water in the bitter January weather.

An army of over 1,000 men requires vast amounts of baggage: tents, ammunition, food, and all the requirements to keep the army healthy. Wagons, which carried the supplies, would have to be driven over primitive roads that were wet and muddy. Each river would present a problem of boggy swamps along the banks.

Tarleton started with rations for four days, but after that his troops would have to forage for food for themselves and for the horses. The countryside was not prosperous, and the inhabitants had little to provide this invading force and even less inclination to share what they did have.

Although Tory scouts were gathering information for Tarleton, the Patriot settlers were not idle. They, too, moved about the countryside watching and waiting. Tarleton's reputation for ruthlessness had penetrated every corner of the upcountry, and it was soon widely known that he was moving closer.

They say that Tarleton's in the highlands
And his British troops are near.
There'll be blood shed in the meadows
When Bloody Ban gets here.
With his troopers riding swiftly,
Their sabers flashing high,
Bloody Ban will give no quarter.
Those who can't escape will die.

The size of his force and the units involved did not escape notice. Tarleton's force was roughly twice the size of Morgan's Flying Army. If Morgan was forced to fight, he needed more men. He needed the backcountry militia. Would they come?

They came.

Col. Andrew Pickens and 150 Long Cane militia joined Morgan at Grindal Shoals about 4 January.

Many more men would be needed, but Andrew Pickens could attract others from near and far. Pickens would be Morgan's choice to command the militia, and he was an excellent choice.

Andrew Pickens had been a fierce fighter in the early days of the war. After Savannah fell, Pickens led his militia and, with Georgia militia under the command of Elijah Clarke, had defeated a Tory force at Kettle Creek. He had taken a parole after the fall of Charleston, thinking the war was over. He had been promised protection for his family and property in exchange for his word that he would not take part in the conflict.

Pickens kept his parole until British and Tory forces razed his home and brutalized his family. Pickens announced to the British that he considered they had violated their agreement and he was no longer bound by his parole. By returning to the action, Pickens and others who had renounced their parole were condemned men. If

Andrew Pickens, much as he would have appeared at Cowpens
(By Benson Lossing)

the British or Tories were to capture them, they would be hanged. In the language of the times, "they fought with a halter 'round their necks."

Pickens, a remote, quiet, and withdrawn man, was known as Wizard Owl. He was known as a taciturn man who rarely spoke and never smiled, but he was a fearless leader in fighting Tories or Indians, and he was known to the militia throughout the area.

The militia who accompanied Andrew Pickens were men of considerable experience. Many had been at Kettle Creek, King's Mountain, or many other skirmishes that had occurred in the backcountry of the Carolinas and Georgia. They were, mostly, riflemen who had fought Indians and Tories in the upcountry and had a great respect for this quiet, fiercely private person, Andrew Pickens.

After Andrew Pickens reported to Daniel Morgan at Grindal Shoals, he left the camp and moved into the upcountry, sending out word that the militia was needed. No one knew for certain where the Americans and British would meet, but it would be in the vicinity of the cow pens where cattle were pastured in the summer and where drovers rounded them up for the drive to markets in Camden and Charleston.

The Wizard Owl has come
To the upcountry to fight.
We know of Pickens' daring
And the Indians put to flight.
He will lead our brave militia

But needs every mother's son,
If the British are to be beaten
And the battle's to be won.
Meet Pickens at the cow pens
Before the British troops appear.
For many more Patriots will die
Unless we stop them here!

The cow pens were well known to all who traveled in the upcountry. Militia had camped there before as the terrain with fresh springs provided a pasture for horses in the growing season. Now it was mid-winter, and the grasslands lay fallow. Still, it was a landmark that could be easily found by travelers.

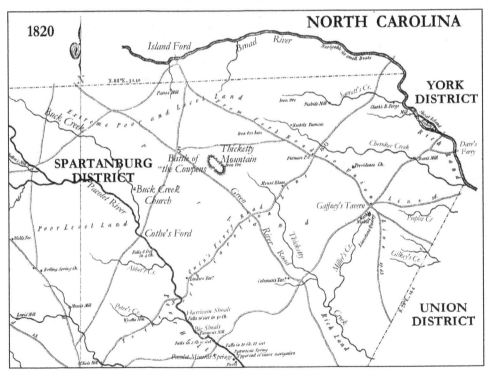

The immediate area around Cowpens, as it looked 39 years after the battle. Most businesses shown did not exist in 1781.
(Adapted from the Mills Atlas map of Spartanburg District, surveyed in 1820)

Although Pickens brought his own militia and could count on many locals to join him, would it be enough? Would the militia respond in great enough numbers to overcome the numerical advantage the British forces enjoyed? The call echoed through the upcountry. Morgan needed the militia. Tarleton must be stopped.

Can't you hear your country call you?
"Come to the cow pens," is the cry.
Morgan needs your brave militia
Else his Flying Army die.
Andrew Pickens' at the cow pens,
And Continentals will be there.
Meet Dan'l at the cow pens,
That brave old Wagoner.
There'll be slaughter in the highlands
If Daniel Morgan fails.
The Carolinas will be lost
If Bloody Tarleton prevails.
For the sake of wives and daughters
Take rifle, shot and powder,
Mount your horse and ride,
Toward the calls which echo louder:

Come to the cow pens!

Come to the cow pens!

Come to the cow pens!

6

THE MILITIA

Since earliest colonization men were required to train as militia, or citizen soldiers, for the defense of the settlements. By 1780 the militia was not considered very reliable and lacked the stature of the regular soldier. This was because their service was sporadic and training less rigorous. Each state had its own requirements for the militia, and usually men reported for thirty or sixty days. Because they were citizen soldiers and not full-time professionals, they were often considered untrustworthy. Indeed, in some cases, they were.

However, in South Carolina and Georgia militia had been reliable in this time when their states were occupied by the British Army with no Continental Army present. Elijah Clarke's militia, known as the Georgia Refugees, had continued the fight in that state.

Thomas Sumter used militia forces to great effect in the midlands of South Carolina and had inflicted serious casualties on the Tories and British. Recently he had encountered Tarleton at the Blackstocks and had delivered a serious blow to that force.

Even now, Francis Marion's militia forces controlled the area between the Santee and Pee Dee Rivers, interrupting the supply routes from Charleston. Marion had many successful conflicts with local Tories and Loyalist troops.

The difficulty for the militia was the manner of fighting. The Continental Army adopted similar tactics to the British, and they fought in an almost orchestrated fashion. The ordered volley of muskets, then the charge with the bayonets was the usual order of battle. The British were well trained in this approach and the Continental Army was training in the same manner.

The backcountry militia, armed with long rifles, could not stand and fight like the Continental soldiers. The rifles were not equipped to mount a bayonet, and the long rifles, although more accurate, required longer to load than the muskets issued to British and Continental soldiers. They understood their vulnerability and, because they tethered their horses near the action, would often ride off if the fighting were not to their liking.

However, these men were not cowards. They fought hand-to-hand with Indians with tomahawks, and they were fearless when they were not at too great a disadvantage. They had inflicted serious damage on Tory and British alike at such battles as Kettle

Creek, Musgrove's Mill, Blue Savannah, Black Mingo, Brattonsville, Blackstocks, and King's Mountain. Yet they fought when and where they chose and appointed their own leaders.

Morgan, greatly outnumbered, needed the militia now, and the call went out through the hill country, and beyond. He needed a much larger force if he were to meet the British on the battlefield. Would they come in sufficient numbers to give Morgan the manpower to stop Tarleton?

They came.

The militia had heard the cry that echoed through the hills, in the valleys, and along the hollows. They rode to meet Morgan and Pickens at the cow pens. Yes, they knew the area, and they rode in from far and near to fight this new threat to their homes and families. Tarleton's troops outnumbered Morgan's troops by two to one and, if Tarleton won, blood would run deep in the backcountry of the Carolinas. No one doubted that.

The militia came in large groups and small groups, but would it be enough?

The arriving men joined with others they knew from previous encounters. Georgia militia, called Georgia Refugees, who had fought Indians and Tories, came without their wounded leader, Elijah Clarke. Clarke and his men had fought with Andrew Pickens at Kettle Creek, and they would fight together again. However, Clarke had been seriously wounded the month before at Long Cane. He sent about seventy-five of his finest riflemen and officers to serve with Pickens.

Both regiments of the Spartan Patriot militia, about 500 men, were called and they came. They were locals who knew the area and, like the others, they knew of Daniel Morgan and they'd fight for him.

The Little River militia, numbering about 200, came with their leader, Lt. Col. Hayes, who had distinguished himself at King's Mountain.

More King's Mountain veterans were among the 200 North Carolinians who arrived with Lt. Col. Joseph McDowell, another hero of that victory. As the militia numbers grew, campfires lighted up the cold night as the men tried to keep warm. And the numbers grew all evening and all night as the militia came.

A few militia cavalry arrived and, although they were few in number, they were determined to fight off this latest British threat. Although Tarleton's cavalry would greatly outnumber the Patriot mounted, the numbers of militia gathering

Typical military garb
(Courtesy,
AmericanRevolution.org)

Typical militia camp scene

at the cow pens gave hope to the assembled fighters that they would prevail.

In the bitter cold, rainy night the men huddled around campfires and ate. They tried to take some warmth from the fires. The regulars who had traveled with Morgan had been briefed, and those commanders knew what was expected of them in the coming battle. The newly arrived militia was greeted by Morgan himself who visited the groups around the fires. He didn't look like a general, dressed in a hunting shirt and without the accouterments of command, except for a sword. But they recognized him: he was a legend, this former sharpshooter who was now a famous general.

Morgan, himself a rifleman, knew their fears. Their long rifles took longer to reload than the muskets carried by British and American regular soldiers. Their rifles also would not mount a bayonet so they carried tomahawks and scalping knives. Morgan understood that these were men of great courage, and they were not reluctant to fight. However, they were vulnerable to a bayonet charge or an attack of horsemen wielding sabers. Tarleton's mounted had the reputation of slashing down militia if given any opportunity.

Morgan knew his success would depend upon the militia's standing firm in the approaching battle. He promised them that his Continental infantry under Howard's command would protect them from the British bayonets. Washington's Continental cavalry would engage Tarleton's mounted troops of the British Legion and prevent a saber attack on the militia.

Morgan outlined the task he expected of them. He asked for accurate fire on the British line, targeting the epaulets and cross webbing that indicated a soldier's rank. In other words, kill the British officers and sergeants. The British mode of battle was an ordered volley; but without commanders, disorder often resulted. That was what had given the Americans the advantage at the Battle of Saratoga. Morgan intended to repeat the tactic here.

From his riflemen, Morgan wanted two volleys into the British line at killing range. This would still place the militia beyond serious danger of the volleys from the less accurate and less powerful muskets of the British. Then the militia was to retire behind the American Continental lines and regroup.

Morgan talked of their great bravery and how, when it was over and the battle won, the old folks would bless them, and the young girls would kiss them. Morgan was known to raise his shirt sometimes and show his men the scarring that washboarded his back from the lashings he had taken from the British as a young man. He might have done that on this cold night before the battle to remind those assembled that he had a score to settle with the British. That score could only be settled if the militia inflicted enough casualties in the British line to even the odds.

Morgan laughed about "Old Ban," but Tarleton, in his mid-twenties, was little more than half the age of Morgan. And Morgan boasted of what they would do to Tarleton in the coming battle. Privately, Morgan was aware of the great danger in fighting this seasoned British force. Although Morgan was committed to a fight to the finish, he understood the peril.

"I'll take this field tomorrow
Or here my bones will lie.
I'll win here," promised Morgan,
"Or at the cow pens, I will die."

The night was bitterly cold and raining. Men huddled around their fires and rested as best they could. Remembering the night later, soldiers recounted that Morgan never slept but prowled around the camp all night, encouraging the men. Some must have wondered if the great general would have the stamina for the coming fight. Sciatica and rheumatism plagued his aging body, and the fighting would be vicious.

Although Daniel Morgan was only in his mid-forties, his body had sustained considerable abuse over the years. He had been lashed viciously, had been shot in the face, had struggled to push bateaux up the icy waters of the Kennebec River, had spent time as a prisoner in Canada. His exploits were many, and his prowess with a rifle was legendary, but age and time had taken their toll.

Could sheer determination keep Morgan in the saddle in the coming fight? What would the morning bring?

7

THE BATTLE

It was early morning, before sunrise, when the men were roused. They ate breakfast of corn cakes that had been prepared the night before. Men fight better on a full stomach. Wagons of supplies and horses of the militia were moved back from the expected battle line. Then the men were moved into position.

The militia line of 1,000 men, most with long rifles, stretched across the field along both sides of the Green River Road. In the cold mist of the early morning they stamped their feet and blew on their hands to ward off the bitter chill. Ahead of the militia line, positioned among the trees, were the Georgia and North Carolina sharpshooters designated as skirmishers.

Finally, the men in the skirmish line saw the first British troops as they exited the woods and moved up the Green River Road. They were Tarleton's own dragoons in their distinctive green jackets. Then came the artillery in their blue uniforms and finally, infantry and horsemen, in scarlet red. Blood red. Over 1,000 British troops were advancing along the Green River Road.

In an effort to determine how Morgan had arranged his troops and how he intended to fight, Tarleton sent his green-jacketed dragoons forward. As they rode up the Green River Road, the skirmishers in the woods took aim and fired on the advancing British troops.

Make every shot count, boys.
See the troopers now skedaddle
Back to their brutal commander
With many an empty saddle.
Make every shot count, boys
And pray with every load.
We'll make the British pay, boys,
Along the Green River Road.

When Morgan's sharpshooters denied Tarleton any chance of reconnaissance, the British commander decided to attack immediately.

One would think that Morgan's reputation should have given Tarleton pause. Shouldn't he have remembered that arrogant British officer, General John Burgoyne, and what had happened at Saratoga? Burgoyne had similar disdain for the Continental Army and contempt for militia. Daniel Morgan had been instrumental in defeating Burgoyne at Saratoga. This same Daniel Morgan had commanded riflemen at Freemen's Field at Saratoga, and they had inflicted

700 casualties on Burgoyne's British army in one day. Shouldn't Tarleton have been more cautious? Shouldn't it have occurred to him that Morgan could do to Tarleton what he had done to Burgoyne?

Perhaps not. It is known that Tarleton was an indifferent student at university. Perhaps he did not have the intellectual discipline to seriously consider what he must have known about past British failures and past Morgan successes. Or perhaps he did not think he could fail. Tarleton was known for brashness and impatience and often underestimated his opponents. Whether through ignorance or arrogance, Tarleton started the attack.

Morgan was ready for the assault. He knew the young officer would not hesitate. Morgan had talked to men who had faced Tarleton before. He studied the British cavalry officer's past actions well, and he knew his enemy. His entire troop placement depended on Tarleton's headlong attack, and he was not disappointed.

While Tarleton dressed his troops in battle line, the militia waited. One thousand militia stretched across the Green River Road. Their commander, Andrew Pickens, knew what was expected of his men. Morgan wanted the first volley at fifty yards, although most of the men in the line thought they could hit their target at a much greater distance. However, their officers moved among them, cautioning them to hold their fire.

Tarleton halted his troops about 300 yards from the

American line and ordered them to rid themselves of all extra equipment that they carried on a march. They kept only the essentials: muskets, bayonets, canteens, and ammunition. Then they formed in their battle line with officers leading their units. There arose from the British line a great shout.

Morgan gave the order for the militia to respond with the Indian halloo, a wild war cry that the early settlers had copied from their Indian enemies. A great roar went up from the militia, a shout that identified these mountain men as those the British called "the yelling boys."

Battle of the Cowpens *(Courtesy, Independence NHP)*

"Give them the Indian halloo, boys,"
Was Morgan's order to his men.
The shout rose along the line
And echoed again and again.
It should have given the British pause
To hear that raucous cheer.
Like Ferguson, they soon would know,
The yelling boys were here.

The British regiments in their splendid uniforms moved towards Morgan's line of militia. Their drums sounded the beat, and the disciplined soldiers marched to the attack. A few British soldiers fell as the sniping continued from the skirmishers, but the British moved forward quickly.

What a line it is before us!
Bright red and blue and green.
Marching forward into battle.
It's a sight I've never seen
Along the Green River Road.

The men on the militia line waited. The British moved within 200 yards.

"Not till they're in killing range, boys. Mind you, aim careful. Take down the officers. Two fires, then we move behind the Continentals. Two fires, boys. Aim careful and give them a belly full of lead."

Come, give me the order to fire,
I've an officer in my sight.
There'll be bloody British bodies
On the Green River Road tonight.

One hundred and fifty yards. The British kept coming. Did they think they were invincible? Or did they expect the militia to turn and run in the face of such an army?

One hundred yards. Still the British were beyond the range of the first volley Morgan had ordered. It must have been a terrifying time as the militia waited in the face of such an army. But they waited, and they held their fire as the British marched steadily toward them.

Due to the contours of the battle site, Tarleton probably never knew how many militiamen were waiting below the rise. Or was he sure that the militia would flee? For whatever reason, the British kept coming and were within fifty yards and still moving rapidly forward when the militia got off that first volley. A few sharpshooters stepped forward to fire, giving the signal for the firing to begin. The initial volley tore into the British line, inflicting heavy casualties, especially among officers and sergeants. Many common soldiers also fell, and the resolve wavered. The line slowed but then moved forward.

Some of Pickens' men reloaded and fired as quickly as possible and inflicted more casualties before the British could respond. Others could not reload fast

Counter attack by the Continentals
(Battle of Cowpens, by Charles McBarron. Courtesy, Cowpens NB)

enough so did not get off the second shot that Morgan wanted. They had done the best they could. Would it be enough?

The British soldiers were trained to attack riflemen with their bayonets, but before that happened, the Continental lines opened, and the militia filed through to the rear to regroup. Now the British line faced the experienced Continentals armed with muskets and bayonets. It is likely that Tarleton not only misjudged the number of militia confronting him, but also had no idea that Morgan's Continental line was waiting for the attack.

Thinking the defenders had been routed when he saw the militia leaving the line, Tarleton sent his dragoons to attack the vulnerable militia. William Washington threw his Virginia cavalry into the fight and forced back the saber-wielding dragoons.

The British infantry, reeling from the devastating fire they had received from the militia, moved forward. The British soldiers had lost many officers and sergeants, but they were not without courage. They stood their ground, exchanging volleys with the Continentals.

Bayonets flashing—
Sabers clashing—
Horses thrashing—
Bones smashing—
Along the Green River Road.

Drums pounding—
Shots resounding—
Men screaming—
Blood streaming—
Along the Green River Road.

Tarleton ordered his reserve unit, the Frasers Highlanders, the 71st, into action. They were to give no quarter, take no prisoners. They moved to try to flank the line.

The squeal of Scottish bagpipes
Sends shivers down my spine.
Their troops come charging forward
Close to our battle line.

Like fiends from hell they charge
With Scots tams upon their head
And wearing tartan trouser
And jackets of bright blood red.

Seeing the danger, Lt. Col. Howard ordered his men to turn and face the side, but the line got confused and started to move backward, away from the enemy. The remainder of the American line, thinking a retreat had been ordered, moved back but in good order. The line marched, trailing arms, reloading as they moved.

Morgan, who seemed to be everywhere, saw the problem and rode swiftly to get in front of the American troops. He saw the solution and instructed the men to turn, en masse, and fire into the advancing British line

Dragoon action at the Battle of Cowpens
(Courtesy, South Caroliniana Library)

when ordered. The Highlanders thought the American line had broken, and they rushed forward to finish the battle. They had been ordered to give no quarter by Tarleton, and killing was their intent. With this one thought in mind they had broken formation and were coming on like a wild mob. Then the Americans turned and fired at point blank range into the advancing British. Howard then ordered a bayonet attack, and the Americans charged into the British line.

As the stunned Highlanders reeled under the sharp steel of the American bayonets, William Washington charged through the British line with his cavalry, creating more mayhem. Then, from the opposite side, Andrew Pickens charged with his regrouped militia. The British soldiers threw down their weapons and fell, some face forward on the ground, in surrender. Others turned and started running back down the Green River Road to escape.

Tarleton saw the Highlanders' predicament and ordered his dragoons to charge, but the unit saw the danger and turned and fled back down the Green River Road. Those dragoons who had cut down many a retreating soldier in previous battles had no stomach for a fair fight, and 250 of them fled the field, to Tarleton's dismay.

With his few remaining mounted troops, Tarleton tried to protect the guns, but it was too late. The gun crew had stayed by their artillery pieces and fought until all were wounded or dead.

The Highlanders expected to be killed since they had

Dragoon swordplay involving Washington and Tarleton
(Battle at Cowpens, by William Ranney c. 1845,
from the Collection of the State of South Carolina.)

intended to give no quarter, but Howard accepted the sword of the Highland commander and gave quarter to the men who surrendered. The killing stopped. It would have been a far bloodier field if Tarleton had won. Slaughter would have been his choice.

With the battle lost, Tarleton turned with his few mounted dragoons who had not deserted him and left the field. Washington pursued him, charging into the group. Washington's sword broke, and a British officer shot at him. The bullet missed Washington but wounded his horse. Because the Continental cavalry was rapidly riding to the assistance of Washington, the British officers fled.

All over the battlefield men were taking prisoners, helping the wounded, claiming trophies. Mounted militia rode off to round up prisoners who were trying to escape.

The battle had lasted less than an hour. The field was strewn with the dead. British soldiers lay in their colorful uniforms in lines marking the harshest fighting. Tarleton had quit the field and left more than 110 dead British soldiers on the ground. More than 200 more were wounded, some mortally wounded. The victorious Americans took 600 British soldiers as prisoners and captured two artillery pieces, thirty-five wagons, 100 horses, and 800 muskets. The British also had traveled with sixty to seventy slaves to attend the British officers. They, too, were captured by the Americans.

Morgan reported twelve dead and sixty wounded, but those figures did not include the newly arrived militia casualties, only those of the Flying Army. Andrew Pickens reported that militia casualties were light.

Morgan rounded up the beaten and wounded soldiers as prisoners, but there was no time for a victory celebration. Morgan knew that he had captured Lord Cornwallis' light infantry, seasoned and trained troops, and Cornwallis would endeavor to get them back. The British commander would only need to rearm them and integrate them into the army he had kept with him. Six hundred men could make a difference in many a battle. Morgan had little time before Cornwallis would move against him and make every effort to overtake him, destroy him, and release those prisoners.

COWPENS ILLUSTRATED

The maps on the following five pages illustrate the course of the battle at Cowpens. The lighter areas represent hills, while the darker areas are low spots. These maps were produced by John Robertson, using the research of Lawrence E. Babits.

Topography of Cowpens Battleground

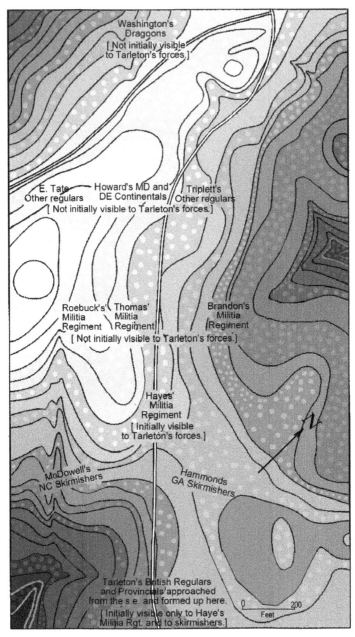

Initial deployment of forces, British and American

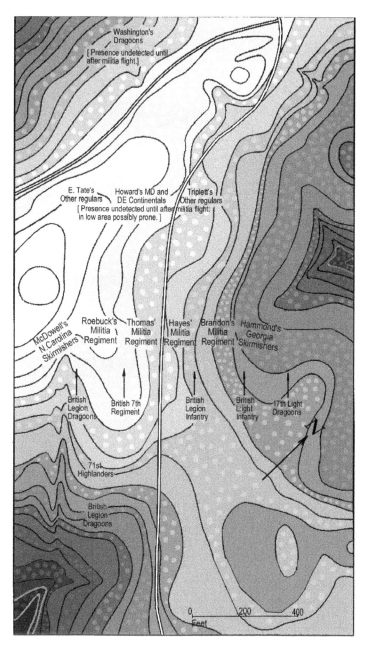

Tarleton's forces advance on the militia line, strengthened
by skirmishers on the flanks.

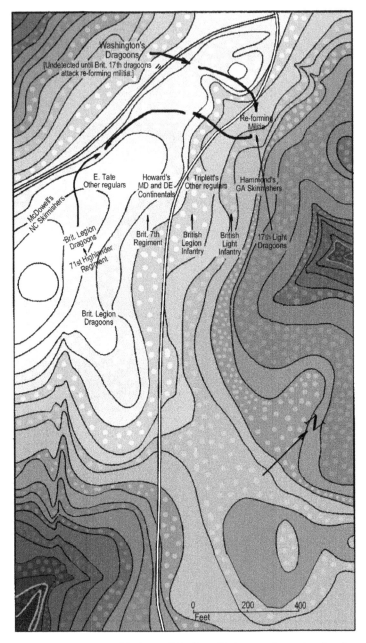

Washington's
Dragoons
[Undetected until Brit. 17th dragoons
attack re-forming militia.]

Re-forming
Militia

E. Tate
Other regulars

Howard's
MD and DE
Continentals

Triplett's
Other regulars

Hammond's,
GA Skirmishers

McDowell's
NC Skirmishers

Brit. Legion
Dragoons

Brit. 7th
Regiment

British
Legion
Infantry

British
Light
Infantry

17th Light
Dragoons

71st Highlander
Regiment

Brit. Legion
Dragoons

0   200   400
Feet

After a costly encounter with the militia line, Tarleton attempts simultaneous flanking movements with dragoons, both thwarted by Lt. Col. Washington.

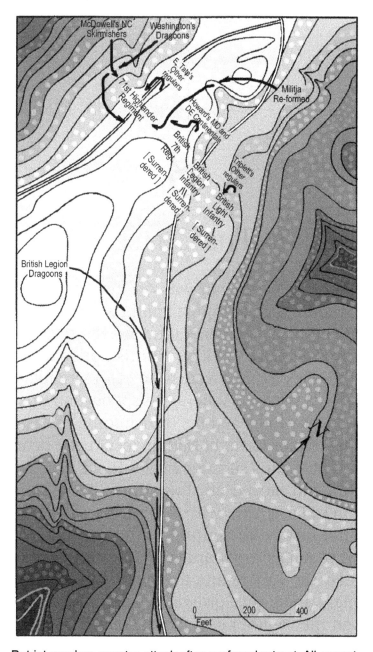

Patriot regulars counter-attack after confused retreat. All except the 71st Regiment surrendered quickly. The 71st is surrounded in "double envelopment."

8

THE CHASE

Before noon Morgan was on the move. Units of North Carolina and Virginia militia were assigned the movement of the prisoners toward the north. There were no safe places to intern British prisoners in the south, so the columns were headed for Virginia. It was crucial that these prisoners be kept beyond the reach of Lord Cornwallis and his British force.

When Major General Nathanael Greene heard the news of Morgan's success, he left Hicks Creek on the Pee Dee and moved northwest into North Carolina. Morgan's Flying Army with the prisoners and Greene's Continentals were reunited. The combined army moved steadily northward, always keeping their force between the Americans accompanying the British prisoners and Lord Cornwallis' pursuing troops.

Even the weather seemed to conspire against the British. Heavy rains made the roads almost impassable, and frequent downpours flooded ferry crossings and

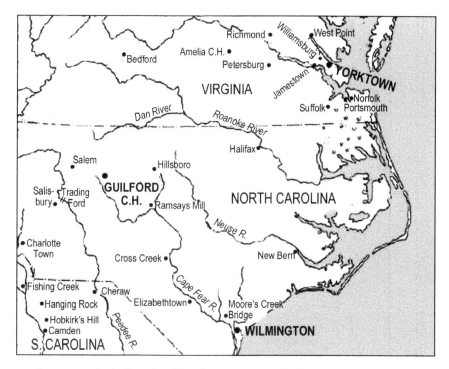

Area map including Guilford Courthouse, Wilmington and Yorktown
(After Lefler)

fords. American militia harassed the British at every opportunity, and the Tories, whose support Lord Cornwallis now needed desperately, were not eager to join the fight.

Lt. Col. Tarleton accompanied Lord Cornwallis but, without the light infantry he had lost at Cowpens, his ability to track Morgan was undermined. Also the wagons carrying the British baggage slowed the march along the red clay roads, muddy from the winter rains. Finally, in desperation, Lord Cornwallis burned his baggage, consisting of tents, wagons, extra clothing, and all things that he thought unnecessary. He kept

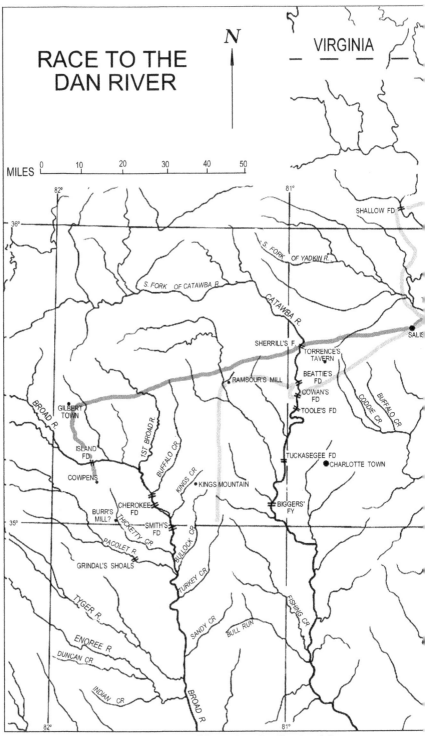

"Race to the Dan River" following the Battle of Cowpens.
Darker gray shows approximate path of the army of Morgan and Greene
Lighter gray shows that of Cornwallis' army.
(Map after Newberry Library and Malone, 1999. Routes after
"Another Such Victory," Baker, 1999)

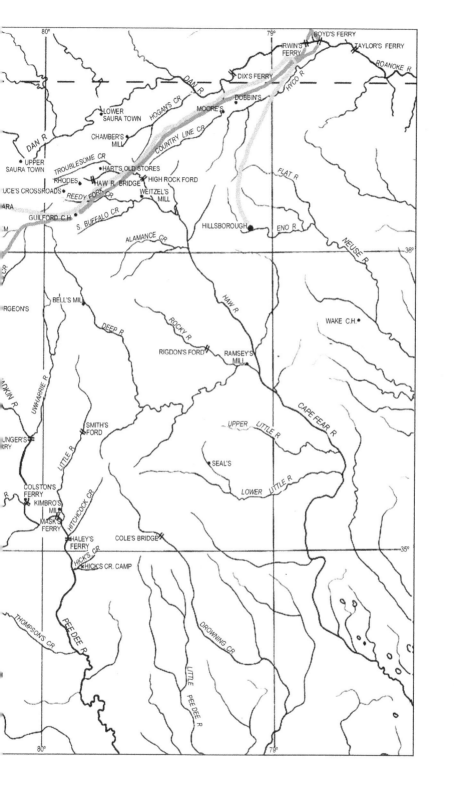

a few wagons to carry salt, ammunition, medical supplies, and wounded. Everything else went into the fire. It was a rash measure to lighten the load of the marching soldiers and to move more rapidly. It did not work. The Americans were able to reach and cross the Dan River into Virginia before Lord Cornwallis could overtake them. Now, in the waning days of a bitter cold and wet winter, the British Army needed the extra equipment that Lord Cornwallis had fed to the fire.

After the British prisoners had been ferried across the Dan, Lord Cornwallis and Nathanael Greene moved back into the interior of North Carolina, and the armies met and fought a bitter battle at Guilford Court House in North Carolina on 15 March 1781. Greene retreated to protect his army, so Lord Cornwallis won the field, according to the rules of war. However, the British lost over a fourth of their troops on that bloody battlefield. Daniel Morgan was not a participant in that battle as the wet and cold winter had crippled him and he was recuperating at Winchester, Virginia.

The weakened Lord Cornwallis moved to Wilmington, North Carolina, to refresh and resupply his troops. He then turned his attention to Virginia and campaigned there, accompanied by Lt. Col. Tarleton. An ailing Daniel Morgan took the field and, with the French ally, Lafayette, harassed the British troops. Again his health failed, and he was transported back to his home on a litter, an uncomfortable stretcher. A lifetime of service to his country had left him with a body racked with pain.

Finally, at Yorktown, Virginia, on 19 October 1781, Lord Cornwallis surrendered his army of 7,000 troops to General George Washington and his French allies. The Southern Campaign, which was intended to win the war for Britain, had failed. The British Parliament sought a treaty of peace to end the hostilities.

In the interim, though, Major General Greene had not followed Lord Cornwallis north after the Battle at Guilford Court House but had turned his attention to the British still in South Carolina. He marched against the British troops at Camden and, at the Battle of Hobkirk Hill, met Lord Rawdon's forces in the field. Again, Major General Greene left the field to the British but inflicted serious casualties on the enemy. Lord Rawdon's post at Camden not only had to contend with the British dead, but with seriously wounded soldiers. Supplies were scarce, especially food and salt. Francis Marion and Lt. Col. Henry Lee, (known as "Light Horse Harry") had cut the British supply lines from Charleston, so Lord Rawdon evacuated Camden. It was evacuation or starvation. Lord Rawdon moved the troops, and many Camden area Tories and their slaves, south to Charleston.

Major General Greene then attempted a siege of Ninety-Six, a British outpost in predominantly Tory territory. Lord Rawdon marched troops from Charleston to Ninety-Six and ended Greene's siege. Then Rawdon evacuated Ninety-Six, moving those troops and Tory civilians to Charleston.

Another long and bloody battle was fought at Eutaw Springs in South Carolina on 8 September 1781. The battle lasted four hours, and the casualties were heavy on both sides. However, Greene's troops left the field but maintained a presence in the area. The British evacuated Eutaw Springs and moved into Charleston Neck.

By 19 October 1781, when Lord Cornwallis surrendered to George Washington at Yorktown, Major General Greene had forced the British from all their outposts in South Carolina and into the area around

Battle of Eutaw Springs, September 1781
(Drawn by Robert Hinshelwood for "Graham's Magazine." Courtesy, South Caroliniana Library)

MEMORIALS TO DANIEL MORGAN AT SPARTANBURG, S.C., AND WINCHESTER, VA.

Left: Morgan statue atop 1881 Centennial Monument, Spartanburg, S.C.

Close-up of Morgan's image at Winchester, Va., memorial.
(Courtesy of Angelique Ruff)

Left: Morgan memorial at his burial site in Winchester. Inscription:

THE PEOPLE OF WINCHESTER VIRGINIA
DEDICATE THIS MEMORIAL TO THE
PATRIOTISM AND VALOR OF
GENERAL DANIEL MORGAN
TO THE CAUSE OF AMERICAN
INDEPENDENCE.

Charleston. Although the British Parliament conceded that the war was unwinnable and started peace talks in Paris, the war still raged on in the backcountry.

For a year after Yorktown Tory reprisals were common, and the Cherokee Indians, led by Tory militia, still threatened the settlers in the backcountry. Patriot militia commanded by Andrew Pickens and Elijah Clarke moved into the Chattahoochee River area and defeated the Indians, ending the Cherokee War in October 1782, a year after the British had been defeated at Yorktown.

The British finally evacuated Charleston on 14 December 1782, taking with them more than 4,000 Tories and more than 7,000 slaves. It took 300 ships to remove the British, their supporters, their slaves, and their possessions, but the war was finally over.

Although Daniel Morgan was not part of this final campaign in South Carolina, he had turned the tide of the American Revolution in the south. He had led regulars and militia and had won a great victory over seasoned British regular troops. South Carolina historian Robert Bass reports of Cowpens that "contemporary British commentators said that Tarleton had lost the battle, that lost the campaign, that lost the war, that lost the American colonies."

9

THE AFTERMATH

When Morgan hurried the prisoners from the battlefield at the cow pens, he left on the field the dead and seriously wounded British as well as his own. He left the field to the militia and to Andrew Pickens. They, and the local inhabitants, took care of the wounded as best they could. Some wounded were taken to shelter in local cabins. Others were cared for in tents. The Americans had no tents but used those the British had dropped when they had prepared to fight.

The wounds were horrible. It is probably not an exaggeration to state that, if a wounded man could not get himself off the field, he would die there. The local inhabitants did the best they could, helping American and British surgeons treat the wounded.

Medical practice was primitive in those days. Puncture wounds made by three-sided bayonets were especially ugly and dangerous. Since this was before the discovery of antibiotics, those dirty wounds often became infected and the soldier died.

Bones smashed by bullets to the extremities required amputation of the arm or leg. Without anesthetic, the soldier underwent a painful ordeal with only, perhaps, some strong drink to dull the senses and a bullet to bite on while the surgeon cut through the flesh to the bone, then sawed through the bone. The stump was often cauterized with hot grease to stem the bleeding. Mercifully, it was a fast operation as the surgeons who attended the wounded on battlefields worked rapidly, and the entire operation was completed in minutes.

Bullet wounds to the body might heal if they were not too severe and the soldier was lucky enough not to get infected. Slashing wounds made by sabers were painful gashes, usually around the soldier's head or upper body. Arms and hands were often wounded as the soldier tried to ward off the saber blows delivered by horsemen. Again, the danger of infection was great as the battlefield was always an ugly, filthy mess.

If a soldier were to escape a wound, there were many other dangers. Camp fever (dysentery) was epidemic, and many died of dehydration. Smallpox was a constant threat as well as yellow fever and malaria. Little wonder the men left as soon as possible and returned to their families. Soldiering was a dangerous business.

This bloody field of victory
Where lately soldiers trod
Strewn with the wreckage of battle

On the cold and bloody sod.
Here wounded and the dying
Lay in the freezing mud.
Can even the rains of heaven
Ever wash this blood,
From the Green River Road?

The militia, who were charged with the care of the wounded and the disposal of the dead, feared that Lord Cornwallis might be traveling in their direction. Within twenty-four hours the militia had departed from the battlefield. Many of the wounded were taken to the few homes in the area where they were cared for until they recovered or died.

But what happened to the dead left on the field? Perhaps the dead were buried on the field where they fell along the Green River Road. That was the usual method of disposal of the bodies. Occasionally, bodies were buried in mass graves. However, tradition has it that, since the cold ground was too harsh to dig, and the weather was deteriorating rapidly, the dead were piled into the wolf pits that dotted the area. Wolf pits were dug to trap wolves, which preyed on cattle.

In any case, the location of those graves, or any graves at the Cowpens National Battlefield, is unknown. But they are surely there, as over 100 were killed at the cow pens along the Green River Road.

In the bitter cold of winter
On a clear and cloudless night

When the battlefield at Cowpens
Is bathed in pale moonlight,
You can hear the sounds of battle
With its suffering once again,
The screams of dying horses,
The prayers of dying men.
There are spirits here at Cowpens
And those spirits do not sleep.
They march the fields forever
For a vigil they must keep.
"Meet Morgan at the cow pens"
Is a cry that will not cease
In the hearts of men and women
Who still fight and die for peace.
Today, when liberty is threatened
And hate and violence rages,
Again Patriots answer a call
Like that which echoes through the ages—
Come to the cow pens!
Come to the cow pens!
Come to the cow pens!
Come to the cow pens!

AFTER THE WAR

What happened to the men who were involved at Cowpens?

Lord Cornwallis was not present, but he commanded the British forces in the south at the time of the Battle of Cowpens. He surrendered his British command at Yorktown. He returned to England and lived to complete a distinguished career in British government. He became governor general of India, the most important post in the British Empire. He died in 1805 at the age of sixty-seven.

Lt. Col. Banastre Tarleton, the commander of the British forces at Cowpens, was among the British troops who surrendered at Yorktown. Born in England to an upper-middle class family, he returned there after his service in the colonies. He was promoted to general and became an intimate of the Prince of Wales. He was knighted and served in Parliament. He died in 1833 at the age of seventy-eight. In England he is considered to be a hero of the American Revolution. Citizens of South Carolina have a different opinion.

British forces at the Battle of Cowpens were taken prisoners. Most were Americans from New York and New Jersey serving with the British Army. After their release, many were evacuated from New York to Port Mouton, Nova Scotia, Canada, where they were settled. Because Canada was a British colony, these Tories were given land grants in that largely unsettled region. To research this group on the web use the term "United Empire Loyalists."

Major General Nathanael Greene was not at the battle, but he commanded the Continental Army in the south at that time. He joined Morgan on the journey north with the prisoners. After the Battle of Guilford Court House, Greene turned his attention to South Carolina and succeeded in his effort to push the British into Charleston Neck before the British surrendered at Yorktown. He commanded at the Battles of Hobkirk Hill, Ninety-Six (siege), and Eutaw Springs and led the Continental Army into Charleston as the British evacuated. In appreciation, the state of Georgia gave him a plantation near Savannah where he made his home until his death in 1786 at age forty-six. He is buried in Savannah.

Brigadier General Daniel Morgan, who commanded the forces at the Battle of Cowpens, served again, but ill health forced him from the field. He was not involved at Guilford Court House but did harass

British troops as they moved toward Yorktown. He retired to his home in Winchester, Virginia, before the Battle at Yorktown. After the war he became owner of a large amount of property in Virginia and in the newly opened territory to the west. During the Whiskey Rebellion he led the government troops to settle the dispute. He served one term in the House of Representatives. He died at the age of sixty-six and is buried in Winchester, Virginia.

Lt. Col. John Eager Howard, who commanded the Continental Infantry at the Battle of Cowpens, was born in Maryland, the child of a wealthy planter. Although not quite thirty years old at the Battle of the Cowpens, he was already a distinguished officer. He survived the war, fighting at the Battles of Guilford Court House, Hobkirk Hill, Ninety-Six, and Eutaw Springs. He was wounded in the last battle but survived. He returned to Maryland and represented that state in the Continental Congress, in the Senate, and served as governor. He died in 1827 and is buried in Baltimore, Maryland.

Lt. Col. William Washington, who commanded the cavalry at the Battle of Cowpens, was a Virginian and a cousin of George Washington, General of the Continental Army. Although not quite thirty when he participated in the Battle of Cowpens, he had already seen much service and was a very capable officer. He fought at the battles of Guilford Court House, Hobkirk

Hill, Ninety-Six, and Eutaw Springs. At this last battle, with his horse shot from beneath him, Washington was wounded and taken prisoner. He was confined at Charleston and married a wealthy young lady of that city, Jane Elliott. After the war William Washington remained in South Carolina and served as a legislator in the state assembly and as a senator. He died in 1810 and is buried at Ravenel, South Carolina.

Col. Andrew Pickens, who commanded the militia at the Battle of Cowpens, was born in Pennsylvania while his family was moving south as part of the Scots-Irish migration. The family first settled in the Waxhaws, where the Great Wagon Road crossed from North Carolina to South Carolina, then moved to western South Carolina. After the Battle of Cowpens, Pickens commanded militia at Guilford Court House, Augusta, Ninety-Six, and Eutaw Springs. After the war he settled along the Seneca River. Although he had fought Indians in his early career, he facilitated the treaties that made peace between the white settlers and the Indians. The Cherokee called him Skyagunsta, the Wizard Owl. He died in 1817 at the age of seventy-nine and is buried in Oconee County, South Carolina.

Not all of the men involved at the Battle of Cowpens survived to enjoy independence in the new nation. For example, **Col. Joseph Hayes**, who had distinguished himself at King's Mountain and had accompanied his Little River Militia to Cowpens, was attacked later that year at Hayes' Station by Tory militia under the command of Col. William Cunningham. When the buildings were set on fire, Hayes surrendered his men only to be butchered by Cunningham, who was appropriately known as "Bloody Bill."

CHAPTER NOTES

Chapter 1: Scots-Irish Settlement

The term "Scots-Irish" is preferred at the present time and is used throughout this writing. The term "Scotch-Irish" is also still widely used. Although many settlers to coastal Carolina came by ship, the pioneers to the backcountry traveled on the Great Wagon Road. Rouse's book is subtitled: *How the Scotch-Irish and Germans Settled the Uplands* and is an excellent source for understanding the migration. Also Leyburn's *The Scotch-Irish: A Social History* not only describes the migration but also has an excellent explanation of the indentured servant.

Chapter 2: Come to the Cow Pens

Although there are several excellent texts covering the Southern Campaign of the Revolutionary War, the situation in the backcountry of the Carolinas is well described in the chapter entitled "The Cherokee War" in *From Savannah to Yorktown* by Henry Lumpkin. Also, see chapters "Trouble in the Back Country" and "More Trouble in the Back Country" in Buchanan's *The Road to Guilford Courthouse*. Another reference, Walter Edgar's *Partisans and Redcoats*, documents the hardships of life in the backcountry. Note: King's Mountain, referenced in Chapter 2 and throughout this book, is now known as Kings Mountain.

Chapter 3: Major General Nathanael Greene

An interesting account of Greene's meteoric rise from common soldier to general officer is found in "A General from Rhode Island," in Buchanan's *The Road to Guilford Courthouse*.

Chapter 4: Brigadier General Daniel Morgan

Several interesting biographies of Daniel Morgan are in print, but Don Higginbotham's *Daniel Morgan: Revolutionary Rifleman* is considered the standard. John Buchanan's remarks on Morgan are well worth reading as he is an unabashed admirer of Morgan.

Chapter 5: Adversaries

Banastre Tarleton's own account of the action in the southern colonies is an interesting, but not totally objective, document. It is difficult reading for a casual reader. A serious reader should follow Tarleton's account with McKenzie's *Strictures on Lt. Col. Tarleton's History of the Campaign*. Mackenzie fought with Fraser's Highlanders at Cowpens and contradicts Tarleton's account of that battle and other engagements.

Andrew Pickens was a Patriot leader of the caliber of Francis Marion and Thomas Sumter but is not so widely written about. There is an excellent account of his life in *Cowpens: Official National Park Handbook*.

Chapter 6: The Militia

Early historians perpetuated the myth that Morgan was greatly outnumbered. A seriously inferior army defeating an army of British regulars had great appeal to citizens of the new nation. Also, the accounts of militia involvement were vague. The research of Dr. Bobby Moss of Limestone College focused on pension applications, muster rolls, private letters, and journals. He has documented participants at Cowpens as far greater in number than previously supposed. The names of those documented are listed in his *The Patriots at the Cowpens*. Research by Dr. Lawrence Babits corroborates those numbers as approximately 1,000. The lists of units, commanders, and numbers of both British and militia forces at Cowpens are included in Babits' *Cowpens Battlefield: A Walking Guide*.

A database of militia participants, based on the research of Dr. Moss and Dr. Babits, is in process and will be available on a National Park Service website at a later date.

Also, the muster rolls of the British units engaged will eventually be available on the website.

Chapter 7: The Battle

Although there are many accounts of the battle, the events recounted here are based on Lawrence Babits' *A Devil of a Whipping* as well as *Cowpens Battlefield: A Walking Guide* by the same author.

Chapter 8: The Chase

Morgan's movement with the prisoners toward Virginia is known as "the race to the Dan." It is well documented in many texts. Pancake's chapter on "Retreat" in *This Destructive War*, is an excellent account, as well as the chapter "Bayonets and Zeal" by Buchanan.

Greene's campaign in South Carolina is well documented in both Lumpkin and Pancake. The numbers for the evacuation from Charleston were taken from Edgar's *South Carolina: A History*.

Chapter 9: Aftermath

The cow pens at the intersection of the Green River and

Island Ford roads are now protected by the National Park Service as the Cowpens National Battlefield. The battlefield is, as it was more than 200 years ago, a serene pasture. Time and erosion have smoothed the rough contours of the terrain, but the visitor can still identify the knoll where a mounted Tarleton tried to determine Morgan's troop placement; stand on the slope behind the crest where the militia riflemen stood and waited for the British; see the swale where William Washington waited with his concealed cavalry; walk the area where Morgan had his camp the night before the battle. The woodlands along the Green River Road are quiet now except for the cawing of the ever-present crows. When the visitors are gone, rabbits, deer, and wild turkeys claim the pasture where Patriot forces defeated regular British troops and marked the beginning of the end of the British Southern Campaign.

See: www.nps.gov/cowp/

References

Babits, Lawrence E. *A Devil of a Whipping: The Battle of Cowpens.* Chapel Hill: University of North Carolina Press, 1998.

Babits, Lawrence E. *Cowpens Battlefield: A Walking Guide.* Johnson City, TN: The Overmountain Press, 1993.

Bass, Robert. *Swamp Fox.* Orangeburg, SC: Sandlapper Publishing Co., Inc., 1974.

Buchanan, John. *The Road to Guilford Courthouse: The American Revolution in the Carolinas.* New York: John Wiley and Sons, 1998.

Edgar, Walter. *Partisans and Redcoats.* New York: William Morrow, 2001.

Edgar, Walter. *South Carolina: A History.* Columbia: University of South Carolina Press, 1998.

Fleming, Thomas J. *Cowpens "Downright Fighting."* Washington, D.C.: U.S. Department of Interior, 1988.

Graham, John. *The Life of General Daniel Morgan of the Virginia Line of the Army of the United States.* Bloomingburg, NY: Zebrowski Company, 1993.

Johnson, W. *Sketches of the Life and Correspondence of Nathanael Greene*. Charleston, SC: A. E. Miller, 1822.

Leyburn, James. *The Scotch-Irish: A Social History*. Chapel Hill: The University of North Carolina Press, 1962.

Lumpkin, Henry. *From Savannah to Yorktown: The American Revolution in the South*. New York: Paragon House, 1981.

Mackenzie, Roderick. *Strictures on Lt. Col. Tarleton's History of the Campaign of 1780 and 1781, in the Southern Provinces of North America*. London, 1781.

Moss, B. *The Patriots at Cowpens*. Blacksburg, SC: Scotia Press, 1985.

Murray, S. *The Honor of Command: General Burgoyne's Saratoga Campaign, June-October, 1777*. Bennington, VT: Images from the Past, 1998.

Pancake, John. *This Destructive War: The British Campaign in the Carolinas, 1780-1782*. Tuscaloosa: University of Alabama Press, 1985.

Rouse, Parker, Jr. *The Great Wagon Road (How the Scotch-Irish and Germans Settled the Uplands)*. Richmond, VA: The Dietz Press, 1995.

Tarleton, Banastre. *A History of the Campaigns of 1780 and 1781 in the Provinces of North America.* Spartanburg, SC: The Reprint Company, 1967.

ACKNOWLEDGEMENTS

This book was prompted by a discussion among teachers from North and South Carolina who served on the Curriculum Committee of a Parks as Classrooms project at Cowpens National Battlefield. As they generated activities for a curriculum guide to help students understand what it was like to live and fight in the Revolutionary War, they articulated a need for a book that would put this important battle in perspective and would address their teaching requirements. Chief Ranger Patricia Ruff suggested that I should write such a book.

I am grateful to those teachers who made many suggestions about what was needed. I would not have undertaken this task without their support.

Superintendent Farrell Saunders and Chief Ranger Patricia Ruff and their staff gave me unwavering support and unlimited access to the resources at Cowpens National Battlefield. Their encouragement is greatly appreciated.

John Robertson is a history buff whose consuming passion is locating sites of the Revolutionary War period and determining how the terrain impacted the events. His familiarity with the geography of the Southern Campaign and the details of the Battle of Cowpens provided valuable maps of the period and of troop movements. I appreciate his attention to detail and his enthusiasm for this work.

Along the way I have been encouraged in my writing by wonderful historians such as Lawrence Babits, John Buchanan, Walter Edgar, and Bobby Moss. Their writings have provided me with an enthusiasm for the period and a better understanding of the events.

Betsy Teter of Hub City Writers Project edited the manuscript and smoothed out many rough edges. I appreciate her careful attention. Chris Lynn was the capable proofreader. Mark Olencki designed the book.

I am grateful to all the students and teachers, family and friends who have supported me in this endeavor.

Christine R. Swager
Santee, SC

The Hub City Writers Project is a non-profit organization whose mission is to foster a sense of community through the literary arts. We do this by publishing books from and about our community; encouraging, mentoring, and advancing the careers of local writers; and seeking to make Spartanburg a center for the literary arts.

Our metaphor of organization purposely looks back-ward to the nineteenth century when Spartanburg was known as the "hub city," a place where railroads converged and departed.

At the beginning of the twenty-first century, Spartanburg has become a literary hub of South Carolina with an active and nationally celebrated core group of poets, fiction writers, and essayists. We celebrate these writers—and the ones not yet discovered—as one of our community's greatest assets. William R. Ferris, former director of the Center for the Study of Southern Cultures, says of the emerging South, "Our culture is our greatest resource. We can shape an economic base…And it won't be an investment that will disappear."